Real Stories. Real Women. Real Faith.

STRENGTH
IN THE STORM

I0528371

30 INSPIRING STORIES

BEATITUDES

STRENGTH IN THE STORM
Copyright © 2024 by Andrea Lende

Cover & Interior Design: Ruth Hovsepian

Paperback ISBN: 978-1-962581-52-3
eBook ISBN: 978-1-962581-53-0

Dedication

To the woman who holds this book in her hands:

May you feel the warmth of God's presence, even in the darkest of storms. Let these stories speak to your heart, reminding you that there is always light, always faith, and always His unshakable love holding you up.

This book is for you—the courageous soul who keeps moving forward, trusting in God's grace to carry you through.

Have not I commanded you?
Be strong, vigorous, and very courageous.
Be not afraid, neither be dismayed,
for the Lord your God is with you wherever you go.
—Joshua 1:9 (AMPC)

Contents

A Note from the Authors

ONE NIGHT, THE APOSTLE Peter and the other disciples sailed out on a calm sea, basking in a gorgeous sunset and reveling in the amazing miracle Jesus had done with five loaves and two fish. After such an exhausting day, it would have been easy to let the gentle waves lull them to sleep.

But a gust of wind picked up, and in rolled dark clouds. At first, Peter wasn't too concerned. He'd fished in many storms from the time he could throw out a net. But the waves grew higher and higher, and then rain poured down. After the first big crash of thunder and flash of lightning, Peter, Andrew, John, and James rowed as fast and furiously as they could toward shore, to almost no avail. For who can possibly row against the fury of a storm?

The others looked to the fishermen to keep them safe, but Peter didn't like the look of those waves ahead. What if the boat sank and they all drowned? Another flash of lightning struck. A man's form strode toward them on the water. It looked like ... could that be Jesus?

Peter handed his oar to another disciple. "Lord, if it is You, command me to come to You on the water" (Matthew 14:28 AMPC).

Jesus held out His hand. "Come!"

Peter stepped out of the boat. He took one careful step, then another. He was doing it! He could walk on water, just like Jesus!

Just then another strong gust of wind blasted Peter with a spray of water. For a second, he took his eyes off Jesus. Suddenly, the water was over his head, and he kicked as hard as he could to the surface, gasping for air. "Jesus, save me!"

Jesus gripped Peter's hand and pulled him to safety. "Why did you doubt me?"

Coughing and sputtering, Peter climbed back into the boat and fell to the floor. The other disciples turned their attention from him and looked at the sky. The placid sea had stopped tossing the boat, and the clouds parted to show a million little stars and one full, bright moon.

With water dripping from his robe, Peter stood up. All of the disciples started talking at once and praising Jesus. "You are the Son of God!"

How often have we found ourselves in Peter's shoes—overwhelmed by the winds and waves of life? Like Peter, we may step out in faith, ready to walk on water, only to find ourselves sinking when the storm around us captures our focus. Just as Jesus reached out to rescue Peter, He's reaching out to us today. Isn't that the hope we all cling to? That in the midst of the storm, our Savior is there to steady us, calm the winds, and bring peace to our hearts.

We all go through seasons when life feels overwhelming, when the weight of our trials, the mountains we face, or the pain we carry seems too heavy to bear. Yet, through it all, one truth remains: *God is still almighty.* His power is greater than any struggle or storm, and His love holds us together when we feel like we are falling apart.

In the pages ahead, you'll find real stories from real women, just like you—women who have walked through fierce storms yet were sustained by God's unshakable strength. Each story is as unique as the woman who shares it, and we believe that as you read them, you'll discover a connection to many of our journeys.

The same Jesus who walked on water with Peter walks beside you today. His compassion knows no limits, and His heart still beats for us with the same tender love.

As you read our journeys, may your heart be strengthened and your spirit refreshed. Let these testimonies remind you that, even in the darkest of days, you are never alone. Our prayer is that your faith will grow stronger, and your courage will be renewed.

No matter what lies ahead, you are never alone. The One who calms the storm, who reaches out His hand, and who lovingly holds you when you feel like you can't hold on any longer—He is with you, and He will carry you safely through.

We pray you find strength in the storm!

STRENGTH IN THE STORM

Real Stories. Real Women. Real Faith.

CHAPTER 1

Dizzying Diagnosis

BRAIN ANEURYSM, FAITH, AND DISCOVERING WHAT'S NEXT

DANG, I'M DIZZY. I feel like I'm falling to the left when I'm just standing still. After months of this woozy nonsense, my ever-patient husband finally encouraged me to get checked out. So I reluctantly made an appointment with the ENT, fully convinced it was just a little vertigo and nothing to worry about.

The verdict came back from the doctor's office: no vertigo, but they wanted to do an MRI just as a precaution to rule anything else out. *Pfft*, whatever. I was the picture of health! This was probably just a giant waste of time.

We scheduled the scan for the following week before I had to leave town for a work trip. Just a quick brain picture, and I'd be on my merry way. No biggie.

Well, let me tell you—that "no biggie" scan turned into the biggest, most terrifying biggie of my entire life. I was merrily driving to our big annual artists' appreciation BBQ, ready to celebrate all the wonderful Christian speakers and influencers we get to work with.

That's when my phone rang. It was the ENT doc. "Hey Mary, the scan is back, and ... you have a brain aneurysm. We've scheduled an appointment with a neurosurgeon to discuss surgery options."

Wait, *what*?! I have a freakin' *what* now? Will I die? What kind of surgery are we talking here? *Brain* surgery? What does this even mean? I was utterly gobsmacked, to put it mildly.

But I didn't have time to process any of those frantic feelings, because, well, I had a BBQ to host and people to appreciate. I pulled it together and powered through the celebration in a weird daze.

A couple of days later, I told my sister—who just so happened to be a neuro nurse—about the two-centimeter aneurysm. She quickly corrected me. "You mean two *millimeters*, right? Not two centimeters?" When I confirmed it was indeed two centimeters, she immediately sprang into action and got me an appointment with her favorite neurosurgeon colleague.

Fast forward to that fateful doctor's visit. The neurosurgeon took one look at my scan and gravely declared, "Yes, that's an aneurysm. And it's a big one."

Okay, I thought. So ... *what's next?*

God's Intervention

You see, up until this terrifying brain aneurysm diagnosis, I was really just coasting along on this very surface-level faith walk. Don't get me wrong, I loved God and considered myself a believer for sure. But I was just going through the motions, checking the boxes without any real depth or authenticity.

I'd been through a tough season not long before landing my dream job at an amazing Christian organization. During those hard times, I desperately clung to God, spending real quality time with Him because I so desperately needed His strength.

But then, when life became easier and comfortable again, I'm ashamed to say I was a little complacent. I still went to church, read my Bible here and there, and said some prayers, but I was just living life on my own terms, completely self-sufficient and not really relying on the Lord like I once did.

Well, this shocking health crisis was a harsh wake-up call. A terrifying reality check that I could not, in fact, "do life" all by myself. As I continued on this harrowing medical journey toward brain surgery, I found myself pulling in tighter and tighter to Jesus, my heart wrapped around Proverbs 3:5–6 (NIV): "Trust in the Lord with all your heart and lean not on your own understanding; in all your ways submit to him, and he will make your paths straight."

In the weeks leading up to the high-risk surgery, I traveled to the West Coast to coach a group of aspiring Christian speakers. I didn't share my diagnosis because I wanted the time to be about them, not me. But you'd better believe I was clinging to God like never before on that trip, silently asking Him, "What's next? What's your plan here?"

After surviving the intense brain surgery, I found myself back in the hospital with a nasty infection on the incision site—this time at my femoral artery, where they'd placed a line to monitor my blood pressure. More uncertainty, more "What's next, God?"

Once I finally made it home to recover, I spent over a month simply sitting quietly, talking to God. I couldn't handle TV, couldn't read books, and could barely hold a conversation. So I just waited and listened, asking the Lord all the questions: Why me? Why now? What's next?

Where God Took Me

Those weeks of enforced stillness, of shutting out the world's noise and distractions, were utterly life-changing. As I pondered and prayed, I felt the Lord gently urging me to take a leap of faith and trust His plan, even if I didn't fully understand it yet.

Deep down, I knew my heart's calling was to help speakers who feel called by God to share an important message. I just didn't know how to start living out that calling. I kept working my amazing job of building tours for speakers and helping kids get sponsored through the power of a well-crafted, powerful message.

Then the pandemic hit in March 2020. In a matter of days, I canceled almost 100 events and personally called every single speaker to share the devastating news that their work had evaporated. My heart shattered for them—the speakers, yes, but also the production crews, the touring teams, the worship leaders. Hundreds of my "work family" were suddenly out of a job.

In that tragic moment when everything changed, I felt God asking me, "What's next, Mary? How can you serve my people in this crisis?"

That's when I was finally ready to take the leap. In July 2020, almost four years to the day after my brain aneurysm diagnosis, I sat down with Jesus and mapped out what became *Take the Stage Podcast*—a way to help speakers without big teams or resources, those just starting or those struggling through the pandemic.

From there, I launched a group coaching program and course to equip speakers with the tools they need to take their message to the world. It was the "What's Next" that emerged from that devastating health crisis years earlier.

I didn't die on the operating table that day because God had something bigger in store. A new calling, a new mission to serve His people and further His kingdom. He just had to grab my attention in a dramatic, life-or-death way first.

Looking back, I'm convinced it took a brain aneurysm for God to finally wake me up from my comfortable, complacent faith walk. To shake me out of simply going through the motions and saying all the right things but not truly living it out.

These days, I'm walking in the "What's Next" every single day, using my lived experiences of struggle, fear, and ultimate redemption to inspire others to take that same brave leap into their God-given callings. And you know what? It's been more amazing, more fulfilling, and more purposeful than I ever could have imagined.

So, if you're feeling stuck in a rut, coasting through life on an okay-but-not-amazing faith, hear me out: Don't wait for a brain aneurysm to wake you up. Start asking God, "What's next?" today. You never know where He might lead you or what incredible plans He has in store.

About the Author

MEET **MARY R. SNYDER**, the speaker whisperer and event guru with over two decades of experience in the Christian events industry. Having been both a speaker and an event planner, she's your go-to guide for navigating the speaking world. Her StorySpire™ Strategy helps both speakers and fundraisers craft the stories that inspire hearts & minds. Mary also uses her storytelling skills to help nonprofits tell their stories through "Impact with Story." Whether you're aiming to captivate audiences on stage or craft compelling narratives, Mary is here to help you take the next step in your journey. Warm, friendly, and full of expertise, she's ready to share her wisdom with you.

Connect with Mary at mary@maryrsnyder.com

CHAPTER 2

Joy and Sorrow Can Coexist

LIFE AFTER LOSS

WHY IS THE DASHBOARD broken?

Why can't I keep my eyes open?

It's so cold. I can't stop shivering.

I struggled to make sense of my surroundings. I have no memory of faces, but I will never forget the voices. "The ambulances are on their way. We are trying to get the helicopter, but with the snow, they can't take off."

"How are we going to get them out of the car? We may have to pull the driver out through the back seat."

We must have been in a wreck.

I turned my head to the back seat to check on Matthew. He was hurt badly.

Could this really be happening?

In the ambulance, I still couldn't keep my eyes open or stay conscious. I saw glimpses of things, like flashing scenes in a movie. "I'm pregnant," I told an emergency worker hovering over me. I was just at the doctor's for my twelve-week checkup and wasn't showing yet. Any medicine they gave me might harm the baby.

"We know," she said. "You've told us several times."

"How is my son, Matthew?" I asked. I couldn't see my husband, but I knew he was alive because I could hear him asking the same question about our five-year-old. The EMTs repeatedly assured us that Matthew was being taken to the hospital. What the voice *didn't* say was that Matthew was okay. I knew he was injured badly. I was worried because he was being taken to a different hospital than my husband and me.

As I was wheeled from the ambulance into the hospital, I saw my dad. "Somebody needs to be with Matthew," I told him.

"Your mom is on the way there now," he said. I imagined my son being alone in a hospital, hurting and not having anyone there with him. It was reassuring to know that Mom was on her way there.

I squeezed my eyes shut, but it wasn't enough to block the bright lights in the emergency room. My head was pounding. My foot and knee were throbbing. The collar around my neck wouldn't let me turn my head. Strapped to a backboard on a gurney, I could hardly move at all.

I was wheeled into a room where I waited to find out the extent of my injuries and the condition of my husband, my son, and my unborn baby. "We're doing everything we can," the doctor said, "but we aren't sure your husband will survive." I signed consent forms for him to have blood transfusions and life-saving procedures.

The obstetrician said, "Your baby's heartbeat is strong. Because your injuries are minor, the baby will likely be fine." I received stitches for a cut near my eye and another on my knee while waiting for X-rays of my back and neck.

"Your parents are here," a voice beside me said. "They want to come in and see you."

What is my mom doing here? She's supposed to be on her way to the other hospital to be with Matthew.

My parents leaned over so I could see them. Dad took one hand. Mom took the other. She had tears in her eyes. "Our Matthew didn't make it," she said.

Not my baby. God help me.

For years, I ran from God in shame and disobedience, but I knew He was the only One who could help me survive the loss of my Matthew.

Nothing happens in God's world by mistake. I'd learned these words in Al-Anon meetings. God was still sovereign. But would He help me after all I'd done to distance myself from Him?

While hospitalized, I felt like I was part of two worlds. In one, I was learning to face the reality that Matthew was dead. In the other, I was dealing with decisions about my husband's medical treatment and the drama that resulted when my choices clashed with my in-laws' wishes. There was hope when the doctors heard my unborn baby's heartbeat and fear when nurses rushed me to ICU because my own heartbeat became dangerously irregular.

From my hospital bed, I made decisions about blood transfusions and other procedures for my husband. I signed the forms for Matthew to be an organ donor, and I used pictures my dad brought in to choose a casket for my five-year-old.

Four days later, on Tuesday night, I was discharged and allowed to see my husband for the first time since the wreck. He was unconscious and on a ventilator. His future was uncertain. On Wednesday, we buried my son. The pastor who preached at Matthew's funeral said losing a child can make us *bitter* or *better*. I wasn't sure I was up for that battle.

The day after the funeral, I sat at my parents' kitchen table. Their neighbor looked me in the eye and said, "You will *never* be happy again."

I shoved my chair away from the table and hurried to the closest place with no people: my parents' bedroom. I looked toward the ceiling and pleaded with God, "Please don't let me be like that. Please don't let her words be true."

How would I put one foot in front of the other? I didn't know.

How would I live each day without my son? I didn't know that either.

Could I face the idea of *never* being happy again? I could not.

For three weeks, I stayed with my parents. I followed my doctor's orders to rest and take care of myself. I didn't spend hours in the ICU waiting room but visited my husband once a day. It was vital for me to rest and take care of myself. At the end of three weeks, I needed routine and some semblance of normal.

At home, fifty miles away from the hospital and the noise of the ICU, the silence was deafening. I listened for the usual five-year-old-boy sounds. They were gone forever. I left his toy cars lined up in his bedroom, just as he had arranged them. I shut the door to his room because I couldn't deal with that yet.

With my doctor's permission, I went back to work. I needed to do something besides sit at home. I needed the distraction, and I needed to have employee leave available to take when the baby came. I visited my husband on the weekends. Four-and-a-half weeks after the wreck, doctors said, "We think he's going to make it." He had a long and difficult physical recovery ahead, but he was going to live.

At home by myself, I grieved. At times, I was angry.

Why did my husband insist we make the trip that day?

Why did the other driver try to pass that car?

Why didn't I push harder for us to stay home?

Why did God take Matthew?

At times, I was scared.

Would my husband recover?

What would life be like for him if he did?

How would our marriage, shaky at best, withstand the grief of losing Matthew?

When I became overwhelmed with sorrow, anger, and fear, I remembered the neighbor's words. *You will never be happy again.* I asked God for help. He heard, and He answered.

In May, five months after the wreck, our daughter, Missy, was born. Joy at her birth collided with the grief of losing Matthew. It was the first time I experienced the strange juxtaposition of joy and sorrow. Happiness and thankfulness for her healthy arrival didn't mean we didn't miss Matthew. Sorrow for our loss didn't mean we loved Missy any less.

In December, the first anniversary of the wreck hit hard. The thin scab that formed during the year was ripped off. Christmas was coming, but the last things I wanted to do were to put up a tree, wrap presents, and celebrate.

I could hide from the joy of Christmas—keep the house undecorated and let grief take over—or I could push through the sadness and celebrate with my six-month-old. We bought a tree, decorated it through tears, and bought and wrapped presents. We rejoiced at Missy's fascination with the lights, the paper, and the boxes. We cried because Matthew wasn't there with us.

God showed me that joy and sorrow can coexist. Celebrating Missy's first Christmas didn't mean we didn't miss Matthew. We *can* experience two opposite emotions at the same time. God also showed me He is faithful and can be trusted. He didn't turn His back on me because of my past disobedience. He didn't withhold His help because of my failures. He didn't shake His finger at me and say, "I told you so." He comforted me, reassured me, and strengthened me.

God placed people in my path to pray for me and share their grief journey with me. "Don't let anyone tell you how to grieve," one friend encouraged me. "Each person's timeline is different. Just don't get stuck in any one stage." This advice was helpful as I experienced anger, denial, and self-pity. Knowing those stages could return—even after acceptance—was a relief.

Other people met physical needs. Friends brought food and called to check on me. People we didn't know well collected cash to help us with expenses. Coworkers walked me through the process of filing insurance claims. God provided for every need. Even the words "you will never be happy again" proved a challenge that kept me from getting stuck in anger and bitterness.

I experienced the truth of God's promise in Psalm 34:18 to be "close to the brokenhearted and save those who are crushed in spirit."

More than thirty years have passed since the day my life changed forever. I still miss Matthew. I think of him every single day. In the beginning, thoughts of him brought crippling, gut-wrenching sorrow, sobs, and ruined makeup. I gave up on mascara for two years. Gradually, the stab of grief became less sharp. Most days, thoughts of Matthew now bring a smile. I wonder what he would be like as an adult. I imagine him helping his grandparents with yard work. I imagine his interactions with his sisters, who never got to meet him. Valerie was born two years after the wreck. She has dark brown hair and eyes, just like her brother. He would have been so proud of Valerie's daughter, his niece, whose newborn pictures look strikingly like him.

Birthdays and anniversary dates still bring tears close to the surface, but most days, thoughts of Matthew include precious memories, moments of wondering what he would be like now, and the bubbling up of hope (certainty) of seeing him again.

I haven't forgotten the days when putting one foot in front of the other took every ounce of concentration and effort I could muster or the heart-piercing pain of the realization that my son was dead.

I remember how God carried me through those days. I recall how He heard my prayers and placed people in my path to share their stories and ways of coping with grief.

Today, my faith is stronger than it was before the wreck. I am not afraid of what might happen because I have experienced God's mercy, grace, and strength in the middle of the worst circumstance I can ever imagine.

Today, I can look a newly grieving parent in the eye and say, "It will get better." I can remind them to ask God for help and suggest they be gentle with themselves in their grief journey. I can share what helped me. I can point them to Scripture, which says God is near to the brokenhearted (Psalm 34:18), and joy comes in the morning (Psalm 30:5). I can assure them that the joy of the Lord is our strength (Nehemiah 8:10).

My parents' neighbor was wrong when she told me I would never be happy again. On the days when I wanted to quit, when I wanted to give up, when I wanted to stay bitter and angry, God used those words to remind me to trust Him and to move forward. He taught me to look for joy alongside sorrow.

I know now God has given us beauty in creation, joy in relationships, and humor all around us. Experiencing those things doesn't mean our grief is over. Laughing and smiling don't dishonor those we have lost. Joy and sorrow can coexist. Living with grief doesn't mean there is no joy. Even after a devastating loss, we *can* be happy again. My friend, if you are suffering, I encourage you to lean into the Lord and seek Him for comfort. He has shown Himself faithful to me, and I know He will be faithful to you. You can trust in Him.

About the Author

MICHELLE RUDDELL IS AN author and speaker. She teaches Bible study at her church and is the co-director of the Waco Christian Writers Workshop.

She is a retired teacher and an empty nester. Her newest and most favorite role is being a grandmother.

Michelle has experienced God's faithfulness through trials of domestic violence, divorce, and the death of her son, Matthew. Through these heart-breaking difficulties, God taught Michelle that joy and sorrow *can* coexist and that it is possible to experience joy even alongside tremendous loss.

Michelle loves to sing along to everything from hymns to praise music. She resides in Central Texas, near her daughters and precious grandbaby.

Connect with Michelle:

Email: michelle@michelleruddell.com
Website: michelleruddell.com
Facebook: Michelle Ruddell

CHAPTER 3

Broken Bond, Redeemed Heart

A STORY OF DIVORCE, STRUGGLE, AND GOD'S HEALING GRACE

I NEVER WANTED TO be a divorced woman, especially after being married for almost three decades. I fought it tooth and nail. But the reality is we were unequally yoked. Yet not always.

When we first married, we were equally yoked under a convenient faith taught from a lukewarm pulpit of ritual and specific Scriptures. We were married based on tradition, not the kind of faith that encourages a relationship and marriage covered by Jesus.

So, our connection changed when I accepted the call to follow Jesus Christ about fifteen years into our marriage. Through an unsettling season, I came to know Jesus; He saved me and radically changed my life.

I refrained from pushing my beliefs onto my husband. Because he had a history of heavy spiritual abuse, I knew that his hardheadedness was going to require a work from God, not me. I prayed and prayed some more. Occasionally, he showed some openness, and then the world showed up and shut his heart down repeatedly.

He was raised with a knowledge of church but not a solid faith to lean on. A "Chreaster" of sorts. His sense of obligation to attend at Christmas and Easter did not mean his heart wanted to be there. We encountered different churches and communities since we lived in many cities. This lack of consistency and his lukewarm desire to trust in a concrete faith in God made it difficult to help him see God's perspective of the world's broken behaviors. His addictions became the stronghold to shutting down a walk with Christ.

He had an unhealthy sexual appetite that was derived from years of abusing pornography. I became the puppet to his masterminding my every move in the bedroom. It was rarely lovemaking and more of a degrading transaction of "if you submit to my ways, I will give you this or that. If not, there will be less financial support and communication until you submit again."

Being young in my walk with Christ, I had a "mentor" whom I confided in. She said, "The Word of God is clear, and you must obey."

The Word she referred to was Ephesians 5:22–24 (NIV): "Wives, submit your-selves to your own husbands as you do to the Lord. For the husband is the head of the wife as Christ is the head of the church, his body, of which he is the Savior. Now as the church submits to Christ, so also wives should submit to their husbands in everything."

What she failed to teach, and I soon learned, is the rest of this Scripture. "Hus-bands love your wives, just as Christ loved the church and gave himself up for her to make her holy, cleansing her by the washing with water through the word, and to present her to himself as a radiant church, without stain or wrinkle or any other blemish, but holy and blameless. In this same way, husbands ought to love their wives as their own bodies. He who loves his wife loves himself" (Ephesians 5:25–28, NIV).

My ex did not love himself, which rippled over to his family and me. His predatory nature was a response to his lack of biblical love from his family of origin and the demons that he allowed to lead him. It wasn't until I built a stronger relationship with Jesus that my eyes were opened to see the toxic parts of the relationship. I was married to a godless man who didn't know a godly marriage. A marriage should consist of purity, respect, and Jesus.

The reality was that abuse, disrespect, and destructive behavior patterns overwhelmed a healthy marriage and partnership. Early on, I allowed it because we began as an equally yoked couple. But as I started to turn my blind eyes towards Jesus's heart, my ex's negative character traits began to overpower the camaraderie we shared and the potential for a healthy partnership. Because of my newfound obedience to God and wanting to know more about Jesus' character, I realized I was in an ungodly relationship, and it was harming me.

However, I was committed to staying obedient to 1 Corinthians 7:12–14 (NIV). "To the rest I say this (I, not the Lord): If any brother has a wife who is not a believer and she is willing to live with him, he must not divorce her. And if a woman has a husband who is not a believer and he is willing to live with her, she must not divorce him. For the unbelieving husband has been sanctified through his wife, and the unbelieving wife has been sanctified through her believing husband. Otherwise, your children would be unclean, but as it is, they are holy."

I stayed hopeful, praying, reading books on unequally yoked marriages and how to save them, and seeking other sources of hope like therapists, podcasts, and, most significantly, godly wisdom. I was unrelenting in my efforts to save this marriage and would stop at nothing to work it out.

There was so much to factor in. In my mind, divorce was not an option. After all, we had two beautiful daughters in critical stages of life. One was a teenager, and the older one was a young adult. They were already facing challenges due to significant growth spurts and the difficulties of navigating a world filled with technological influences. I didn't want to add to their struggles. I firmly believed that a broken marriage would hinder their development. Their father came from a broken marriage, and I witnessed the devastation it caused. Although my then-husband was not walking with Christ, I thought it was my role to tough it out for the sake of my children, my family, and the covenant I committed to.

There were moments, days, and weeks when I thought we would survive. But it wasn't until 2022, when the Lord showed me it was time to stop fighting. This was His battleground, not mine. Here is the timeline:

- In August 2022, my husband lost his job.

- In December 2022, my husband, reluctant to find a job, told me we were out of money and had to sell our home.

- In February 2023, the day before we moved into our rental home, my husband told me he was not moving with my youngest daughter and me, and he wanted a divorce. My oldest was already living on her own.

I was blindsided by what I thought my year and future would look like. Instead of excitedly moving into a new season with my husband and daughter, I was moving into a 3000-square-foot home as a single mom.

My biggest fears came true. I was on my own. My life partner moved away to another state, and I would have to figure out this "life" thing independently. In the marriage, I had leaned on him for everything. Although he did his part by providing financially, I did all of the rest. We were friends who talked, shared dreams, troubleshot work frustrations, binge-watched shows, ate dinners together, and lived life. Despite our massive differences in faith and worldviews, we did life together every single day.

So many questions rotated through my mind. Why would God allow this? Why didn't my ex fight for me and our marriage? How could he do this to our children? How dare he move away and leave me to pick up the pieces of this broken mess?

I felt like I was walking through the valley of the shadow of death. The first few weeks into many months were numb. Divorce took me through a series of emotions. I had no choice but to be still and grieve. After all, this was the death of a twenty-seven-year marriage. Time was not only of the essence but became a critical part of growth and renovation.

Grief is complicated, and needless to say, I went through the five stages of grief thirty or more times. But the beauty from ashes became an abundant covering of God's grace, mercy, and endurance—most profoundly, the clarity of my ex's choice to leave the marriage. Of course, he couldn't be around me. He was living in sin and darkness, and the light of Jesus Christ must have been burning the retina in his eyes.

The most impactful revelation came during a heavy grieving—crying out, if you will. The Lord said this to me:

Jodi,
Get out of the way!
Be still and heal. I know the desires of your heart. I'm working through your pain. It will not be forever.
I have your family and sorrows under my complete control. My promises are true and will prevail. I'm building your ministry to more than you could've ever imagined. Stay close to me and meditate on Proverbs 3:5–6.
I love you!
Father God.

It wasn't often that I heard from God. In fact, I had never heard anything as clear and detailed as this. It was so encouraging and hopeful. It didn't change my circumstances, but it did change my posture as I walked through what needed to be a year-long grief process with faith, hope, and love. This message from God showed me I was on track with His will for my life. Although the valley was dark, complex, and filled with emotions, He promised to walk alongside me. He promised to be my rod and my staff. He promised to comfort me. And He did!

Ironically, my biggest concern wasn't whether I would disappoint my family or my children. I was most concerned about disappointing God. I understood marriage was a holy matrimony and a covenant that He held to His highest standard. Scripture says that God hates divorce (Malachi 2:16.) During the first few weeks, I needed to deep-dive into God's word to ensure I was not accountable for the follow-through of my ex's decisions. I needed to be assured that no matter what, I was in line with God's Word.

I found tremendous solace in this particular Word of God: "But if the unbeliever leaves, let it be so. The brother or the sister is not bound in such circumstances; God has called us to live in peace" (1 Corinthians 7:15, NIV).

There it was—as clear as day—the freedom I was praying for, even though I thought freedom was actually in the marriage. But it wasn't a peaceful marriage. It had moments of peace but years of chaos. It had moments of fun but years of abuse. It had moments of love but years of hatred. I started to learn what unequally yoked really means.

In marriage, being "unequally yoked" is like pairing two oxen of different strengths or sizes to pull a load. If they don't match up well, the stronger or taller ones drag the other around, and they go in circles instead of moving forward. In the same way, if a married couple isn't on the same page with their faith, values, beliefs, or goals, it can create tension. Instead of working together smoothly, they might feel like they're pulling in different directions, making it hard to progress together. This was mine to a tee once I learned about a godly marriage. Before this, I was comfortable being dragged around. I lived with the tension. I was secretly hopeless about my future.

Through the Scriptures and witnessing godly marriages, I learned that a marriage centered around Jesus relies on prayer, trust, belief, and hope. When Jesus isn't in the center, worldviews become the resource. In my situation, the world was my ex's resource for hope. I am pretty confident these are the lies my then-husband believed: "Leave the marriage, and you will find happiness. You two are not compatible, and she is too Jesus-freaky. You don't have to buy into her faith. Just create a new life where you will find peace. Divorce is typical, and this marriage didn't work out. Move on."

Those are typical lies from the enemy.

I found incredible perspective in 2 Corinthians 4:8–9 (NIV). "We are hard pressed on every side but not crushed; perplexed, but not in despair; persecuted, but not abandoned; struck down, but not destroyed." Despite feeling over-whelmed and battered, this Scripture showed me resilience in God's sustaining power. I started to trust in His promises of perseverance and triumph through trials with the foundation of faith and hope.

Of course, when a marriage breaks up, it is a hard-pressing situation. But it didn't crush me because I had intentionally walked with Jesus for years. I understood that life is hard, as Jesus so eloquently tells us in John 16:33 (NIV): "I have told you these things, so that in me you may have peace. In this world you will have trouble. But take heart! I have overcome the world." I could look at my then-husband when he left and say, "You disappoint me." (But in my heart, I understood why he was leaving me.)

I spent a lot of time being perplexed during this time of grief and restoration. Many days, I didn't know if I was coming or going. But even during the darkest days, God made things very clear, which kept me from despair because I serve a God who provides peace that surpasses all understanding. This divorce was no different, and God did not disappoint because He is not the God of confusion. He is the Prince of Peace.

A man leaving a woman for her faith? That is first-world persecution in its most extreme form. Yet, never did Jesus abandon me. Not once, not ever. He was there through the tears, the anger, the fear, the worry, the uncertainty. He became my bridegroom.

Any life-altering situation will strike you down for a little bit. For some, it may be weeks; for others, it may be years. But if we allow it to destroy us, we miss out on His purpose for our lives. We may not see the bigger picture of what God is doing in our lives, but if we praise Him through the storms, trials, and hurts, He restores us and redeems what is lost. He gives us a glimpse of what an abundant life could look like through him. Jeremiah 29:11 tells us, "'For I know the plans I have for you,' declares the Lord, 'plans to prosper you and not to harm you, plans to give you hope and a future.'"

God encourages us to walk through life with a godly perspective: Even though another storm may be brewing, I have Jesus, who is the way, the truth, and the life. That brings me such peace. Through my hard divorce season, I clung to the promise in Romans 8:28 (NIV): "And we know that in all things God works for the good of those who love him, who have been called according to his purpose." I found comfort in Psalm 34:18, which tells us that the Lord is close to the brokenhearted and saves those who feel crushed in spirit.

I received these messages of comfort from the Lord, urging me to "be still and heal through Him." He started the message with, "Jodi, get out of the way" because He knew I would take the path of least resistance. God had another plan, and I needed to get out of the way so He could bring it to fruition.

His message reminded me of His promises to cover us with His feathers, where we will find refuge and, most hopefully, restore us for the future. God's message brought me profound comfort and strength. It still does. I have it written down and tacked up on the wall in my office.

God taught me that this is a part of life, and we don't have to like what happens to us. We live in a broken world. The Bible is very clear about that. Yet, it's not what happens to us; it's how we allow God to handle it.

Isn't He so good and faithful? He has not failed in any of His promises. Although the marriage ended, my ex and I are amicable, and this divorce was bearable—not because of my ex-husband but because of God. His grace was and is continuously sufficient for every day I live and breathe.

About the Author

JODI HOWE LIGHTS UP any stage or microphone with her dynamic energy and heartfelt messages. As an accomplished author and award-winning podcaster, she shares her wisdom and insights on her show, "The Air That I Breathe," reaching audiences around the world. Jodi's vibrant personality makes her a sought-after speaker and emcee at annual conferences.

Passionate about writing, Jodi creates inspiring blogs and prayers that encourage Kingdom living. With decades of experience in the music industry, she understands the transformative power of music and shares this love as a member of her church's worship team and as a vocal coach.

Outside of her professional life, Jodi cherishes her role as a devoted mother to her two children and enjoys caring for her lazy cat. Based in Cary, North Carolina, she embraces a life full of creativity, purpose, and connection.

Connect with Jodi and follow her at jodihowe.com

CHAPTER 4

Overcoming Addiction

POPPING THE CORK PRODUCED a familiar sound. The fizzy pink liquid smelled enticing, like sweet fruit in an orchard. Pouring previously unopened wine down the kitchen sink had become frequent, yet it still seemed wasteful. The soft beams of light from the window above the sink appeared to focus on the glistening cascade as it disappeared.

Determined to quit drinking, I got rid of two bottles of my favorite wine, and hearing the gurgling sound as the wine spilled down the drain reminded me that this was not the first time. I had done this before while making a promise to myself not to bring more wine home. I wondered if this would be the time I could finally break free from a hidden addiction I never imagined I would have. Alcohol consumption was frowned upon not only at my church but also in my family.

The room fell silent as the last drops of wine swirled down the sink with a final gurgling sound. The corks were already disposed of, and the bottles on the kitchen counter were empty. Once I discarded them, removing them from my view, I might be free of this secret—or would I? After leaving the kitchen and feeling satisfied (yet unconvinced) that I had done a good thing, I settled into my favorite living room chair, propping my feet up on the footstool. Unannounced, mild anxiety about not having a glass of wine later in the day crept into my psyche. Almost in panic mode, I envisioned the empty bottles. As I calmed myself, I thought about the bigger picture of my addiction. There was much to ponder.

I went from being a nondrinker my entire life (except for some teenage shenanigans) to being a closet drinker—both literally and figuratively—in my early fifties. While at a routine doctor's appointment during that time, the doctor asked if I was drinking. I explained I had only started a few years earlier, hoping to relieve my heartaches temporarily. He almost fell off his chair laughing. "Most people are quitting at your age, not starting!"

I reflected on my father's struggles with alcohol addiction before he found faith in God, met my mother, and became a nondrinker. Even though my dad has since passed away, I still felt a sense of shame, despite knowing he wouldn't judge me. It saddened me to think about how he would feel, though, if he knew about my addiction. I pondered that maybe I was genetically predisposed to alcoholism, even though I hadn't consumed alcohol until recently. It was as if I had been a sober alcoholic all along.

Although unjustified, I understood how I ended up at that point in my life. My journey was complex, marked by a rocky relationship with my mother, struggles with anxiety and depression, experiences of rejection, low self-esteem, a continual need for validation from others, and a series of poor choices. During that time, while striving to do better, I gained insight into codependent and narcissistic individuals and relationships. I realized for the first time that I had encountered this type of turmoil and conflict for a long time. Then, after facing the trauma of separation and divorce, shame was a constant presence.

I resorted to alcohol to avoid confronting my responsibilities and to escape my sense of being an utter failure. Instead of being accountable for my actions and pursuing healthy alternatives toward gaining emotional and mental wellness, I chose to dull the pain by drinking, thereby exhibiting a victim mentality. Initially, it was a temporary solution to numb the pain in my heart, but even after moving into my own place after the divorce, I continued to drink alone at home and in secret.

I found alcohol addiction to be like:

- Waltzing with a porcupine—sensational at first, then as familiarity increases, the dance becomes prickly and painful.

- Loving and hating a best friend at the same time.

- Bringing home a cuddly bear cub, and it becomes your boss as it grows.

- Starting in the driver's seat of life, slowly losing control, and moving to the back seat.

Finally, I knew deep in my heart, mind, and soul that enough was enough. I sensed an urgency to quit drinking as I was increasingly justifying and hiding my behavior, feeling powerless to change. I experienced worsening headaches, anxiousness, and more shame.

What about my Christian faith? I wondered what God had to say about this unhealthy behavior. Did He understand, or had He given up on me because I should have known better at my age? Was my falling off the wagon more of an emotional and health issue than a spiritual one?

I dug into God's Word to find answers to these questions. I discovered God still loves me as His daughter and always will. His Word tells me He will never love me less because of my mistakes, poor choices, or lack of sound judgment. Romans 8:38–39 reminded me that nothing can separate us from God's love.

I prayed, asking God to forgive me and help me make better choices, one day at a time. Yet it was an uphill battle, with doubts and setbacks. It seemed that hour by hour and day by day, I was confronted with a trigger to lure me into just having one more glass of wine. After all, what would one more drink hurt? I found that freeing myself from my addiction was a battle I had to win in my mind, understanding the only drink I had to give up was the next one. I would also tell myself that I would not drink today, maybe tomorrow or next week, just not today. The next day, I told myself the same thing. In my mind, it was easier to quit one day at a time instead of forever. Each day, I strove to improve, and it became easier. I relapsed and felt discouraged, but I tried again—one day, sometimes one hour, at a time.

In addition, instead of planning how and when I would enjoy a glass of bubbly, I mentally went through all the reasons why I should not. Some were practical: The wine was expensive and caused weight gain, especially around the waist, which I was trying to lose.

After much determination, prayer, and resolve, I gingerly but confidently began making better choices and decisions toward being alcohol-free. Now, my only unhealthy addiction is coffee.

I could see that alcohol, when initially consumed, seems to be a calming solution to anxiety and an escape from adverse circumstances. However, after becoming addicted, it causes more personal destruction, isolation, and stress. Unfortunately, some personalities have more of an addictive bent than others. Many available addiction possibilities present themselves to us daily, and we must be proactive in identifying and curbing temptations. More diligence in being aware of our weaknesses in this area, taking preventive measures, and practicing self-control can subdue unhealthy choices regarding anything that could become an addiction for us.

If you find yourself feeling ashamed and floundering in the hidden hallway of one or more addictive behaviors, know that you are not alone and not destined for a life of failure and victimhood. Your addiction may be different from mine, but be encouraged and believe you can overcome it, regain your health, and find joy and purpose in your life once again. As one who has been there, I urge you to take that first step to freedom, even though you may feel apprehensive and anxious. You are stronger than you believe. It will not happen overnight, but you will succeed with one choice and decision at a time, regardless of how insignificant they may seem. You may feel like you are taking one step forward and then two or three steps back. That is okay! Give yourself some grace. The journey and result of freeing yourself from addiction is worth the hard work and determination.

Some ways to help you achieve success:

- Plan alternative ways to relax or unwind.

- Spend more time with others who inspire you to abstain from your addiction.

- Avoid being alone when you feel discouraged.

- Do not drive by locations that trigger you unless necessary.

- Give yourself healthy rewards after small victories.

- Know when you are most vulnerable to a relapse and plan to do something constructive instead.

- Remind yourself, often, that you are gaining control instead of losing it.

In addition, I encourage you to examine any addictions you struggle to be free of and bring them to the Lord in prayer. Ask for His help in overcoming them and the associated feelings and emotions. To be delivered from an addiction of any kind is freeing and feels like we have shed a great weight off our shoulders that had controlled us.

In Exodus 20:3, we are commanded to worship only God and to have no other gods or idols. Addiction can be an idol and can master us, causing us to elevate the addiction to a place of prominence. In doing so, we tend to sacrifice things that are important and valuable to us, such as our families, jobs, and health, as we feed a damaging addiction.

"Don't be drunk with wine, because that will ruin your life. Instead, be filled with the Holy Spirit" (Ephesians 5:18, NLT). This admonishment is not because God is a killjoy and wants to ruin our chances of having a good time. He wants the best for us, and drunkenness is not the best. A Spirit-filled life is much more rewarding, and time with God is so much more amazing when not feeding an addiction.

Although Jesus' first miracle in the New Testament was turning water into wine, the text indicates that this was for a wedding, and the wine symbolized family status at the time. There is no indication that Jesus condoned addiction or drunkenness. The story is found in John 2:1–11. When we turn to our addictions instead of leaning on God, it deeply affects our hearts. We may not realize it, but we're walking a path that leads us away from the peace and life God offers, moving toward something that ultimately harms us. Yet, God's heart for us is so much more. He longs to lead us down a path of freedom, the kind of freedom only Jesus can give—the freedom we all deeply desire.

God is merciful and patient with us. Although we may have habitually made unwise choices, He forgives us when we repent and helps us do better. He is on our side and wants only what is good for us. As we rejoice in God's work in our lives, He remains faithful to us with every decision we make, helping us win our battles. Our faith increases as we see Him work, preparing us for the good things He has planned for us once we are free from addiction.

In Matthew 22:37–39, Jesus teaches us the greatest commandment: to love God with all our heart, mind, soul, and strength, and to love our neighbors as ourselves. When we struggle with addiction, addictive substances and activities become idols that take the place of God in our lives. But God, in His love and mercy, invites us to place Him back where He belongs—on the throne of our hearts. No idol, no addiction, can ever fill the deep longing within us. Only our Creator, who knows every part of us, can truly satisfy our souls.

God's love is *greater* than our brokenness. No matter how far we've strayed, His love reaches further. You can trust Him to lead you gently out of addiction and into the freedom Jesus gave His life for. This is the true joy and peace He wants for you—a life where His love fulfills every desire and longing.

> The thief comes only in order to steal and kill and destroy. I came
> that they may have *and* enjoy life, and have it in abundance (to the
> full, till it overflows).
>
> John 10:10 (AMPC)

About the Author

PATRICIA J. DOUCET ENCOURAGES women to never give up on aspiring to be the women God created them to be. Her *Beautifully Restored* ministry inspires women to bravely take the next step toward restoration and wholeness.

Patricia is a Bible college graduate, storyteller, author, inspirational women's speaker, artist, and pianist who has written two devotional books:

Coffee Chats: 30 Restorative Devotions for a Broken to Beloved Journey (2023)
Coffee Chats: 30 Reflective Devotions for the Marvelous Middle Years (2024)

She has three adult children and lives in Nova Scotia with her husband.

Connect with Patricia:

Website: patriciajdoucet.com
Email: pat@patriciajdoucet.com
Instagram/Facebook: @patriciajdoucet

CHAPTER 5

Loneliness Is a Journey, Not a Destination

I STOOD AT THE picture window, looking at the familiar scene in the driveway, thinking, "Another long week is coming. I'm so lonely." My little two-year-old daughter was in one arm, leaning her sad head on my shoulder, while my three-year-old son stood on the windowsill beside me, embraced in my other arm, leaning hard on me. Tears streamed down my face as we watched my husband back out of the driveway, tears glistening off his cheeks as well. His last words to the kids before he walked out the door were, "Alright, kids, Daddy's headed to his revival. I'll call you, and I need you to pray for me and the people who need to hear about Jesus."

This routine repeated itself for many months, and the week's unfolding could be almost predicted. We followed a set schedule: wake up, eat breakfast, play or watch cartoons, get dressed for the day, play outside when possible, and then it was time for lunch. Afterward, indoor activities, followed by going outside once again, chasing each other, and playing with friends. We shared snacks, and more play followed. Then it was time to come inside for the evening and get ready for dinner, baths, snuggle time, reading, and off to bed with prayer time and goodnight kisses. There were only a few callbacks for a drink of water or concerns about monsters in the closet. A few more kisses and all was well as we closed our heavy eyes for a good night's rest.

Loneliness was most felt at night when the house filled with a calm stillness, and the only sounds were the soft breathing of my two sleeping children. I missed my husband's warmth and presence during these moments. His absence cast a shadow, especially when the day's chaos settled into quiet loneliness. To cope, I found comfort in little rituals: a hot cup of coffee—thankful it didn't keep me awake, the pages of a book transporting me elsewhere, and God's Word giving strength, calming my fear, and granting me courage for another day. Though these small acts never replaced his physical presence, they offered a semblance of comfort and connection, reminding me love transcends distance and time zones.

I believed God wanted this for our little family, and I made peace with it. I stayed home with the kids while my husband, Edsel, went out to share the message of the gospel of Jesus Christ. As Charles Dickens famously wrote in *A Tale of Two Cities*, "It was the best of times, it was the worst of times." I felt a deep sense of disconnection and sadness in my heart. When I spoke to others about it, I found myself using all the right "church words," but living out those words proved challenging.

It was becoming all too clear. I was on a journey, finding my place of service to the Lord. As a teen, I surrendered my life to "full-time service" (that's what we called it in those days). I wanted to be used by God to draw others to Christ. The path God planned was less than clear to me then, but I never doubted His calling on my life. I imagined myself hopping in the van as we traveled from church to church. But then reality hit. We did try traveling with the whole family a few times. You talk about life experience; God spoke loud and clear.

On one occasion, we loaded up the van with everything (clothes, kids, snacks, toys, sound system, etc.) and headed to Illinois to lead a revival with a wonderful church family. We thought, "How exciting!" Before we even had a chance to meet the people on Sunday morning, I realized while checking into the motel I didn't bring the decongestant medicine the kids were taking. So, the gracious pastor's wife called the pharmacist and got us what we needed. Thank the Lord! You can imagine that, as a mother of two small children, I was wound as tight as a drum.

Finally, it seemed like things were looking up. Wrong! As we settled in for the night, and everyone was sleeping, I woke up to check on the kids in the bed next to ours. All was well. But when I turned to crawl back into bed, there was a distinct crackle in my neck. I couldn't turn my head; it locked up. It's funny thinking about it now, but let me tell you, it was not funny then. Eventually, I realized I had to awaken my sleeping husband. Bleary-eyed, he saw the fix I was in. My left shoulder was hunched up nearly to my left ear. He tried massaging it, and we did everything possible—but we had a problem. After a few hours, it was time to get ready and head to church. I tried to manage our two little ones, walking like the Hunchback of Notre Dame, all the while explaining to each passerby, "I'm not usually like this!"

So, guess what? Yep, another call for medical help. Thankfully, there was a doctor in the church. He prescribed muscle relaxers and pain relief tablets, and I was good to go—or so I thought! The pain subsided within forty-five minutes of taking the meds, and my shoulder muscles began to relax. But that's not all that relaxed. It turns out that taking strong meds on an empty stomach is a bad idea. I was happier than I should have been.

I dropped the kids off at the nursery and was pain free and loose as a goose. All I could think of was how happy everyone seemed. Church started. The dignified pastor greeted everyone and shared a few prayer requests. I've attended many prayer meetings, always behaving as a mature adult, but for some reason, these prayer requests tickled me. I started giggling. I couldn't stop. Everything seemed hilarious. The other evangelist's wife seated beside me touched my hand and whispered, "Judy, shhh... you've got to stop giggling." I have enjoyed reliving these memories, but God used those frantic times to guide me in His loving, gentle way.

During the revival week, something changed inside me. I realized I was putting unfair expectations on my young children, expecting them to act like adults. God spoke to my heart. It was as if He was saying, "Judy, you need to stay home with your babies and show them Jesus. You are not alone. I am with you, and I have a plan for you in this season—and for the next." At first, I wanted to argue and tell God my plan was better. The struggle was real, but I soon realized I needed to surrender my way to His. My remedy for loneliness proved to be no remedy at all.

God used this and other experiences to remind me that overcoming loneliness begins with realizing we are not alone. As Christians, we have a personal and intimate relationship with God, and He wants us to embrace this relationship, which is what I have done. He wants us to allow His Word to fill our hearts and minds. With small children, I needed to be intentional and plan ways to connect with others. God provided special times in His Word, and I grew in my faith and relationship with Him.

Most importantly, I became more involved with my Christian friends in my church family, actively networking with other young mothers and sharing our lives as moms of littles as we moved forward in our Christian journey. I discovered a love for cooking and sewing, and both of these brought great joy. Battling loneliness was a process of personal discovery and letting the Lord lead me to a happy place in my heart. I was doing exactly what He wanted me to do, and that made me happy.

While Edsel was away on his travels, I learned and found joy in everyday adventures. Some days, I had to dig deep but realized I was growing spiritually. During his absence, I planned my weeks, taking on various projects. Some were small organizational tasks, but one involved cutting a hole in the wall using my husband's circular saw. It was a memorable moment when he realized I installed a medicine cabinet upside down. It opened the wrong way. His reaction was priceless, and he graciously left it just the way it was and decided to fill in the little spaces around the cabinet.

At night, to ease my loneliness, I read Scripture, meditated, and prayed about the events of the day and the upcoming day. I left my Bible open on my husband's pillow and turned to a comforting verse. One night, I left it open to Isaiah 41:10

(NKJV), "Fear not, for I am with you; be not dismayed, for I am your God; I will strengthen you, yes, I will help you, I will uphold you with My righteous right hand." Through it all, I grew in my faith.

Overcoming loneliness is a gradual process. I said to myself, "I'll get over this. When my husband is home, I'll be happy. But I'll just feel lonely when he's not here." God is faithful and spoke to my heart, reminding me of a familiar verse in James 4:14 (NIV): "What is your life? You are a mist that appears for a little time and then vanishes." God spoke clearly, "Judy, are you going to waste all those days when Edsel isn't home and focus only on yourself? You have a mission right in front of you—your children." The Lord spoke my language. He understood my thoughts. He knew exactly what to say to wake me up and refocus my daily thoughts not on myself but on the purpose and plan He had for me.

Loneliness impacts almost everyone. It's something we all experience at different stages of our lives. Certain circumstances make us feel disconnected and over-looked, such as parenting challenges, divorce, losing a spouse, changing jobs, moving to a new place, or taking on caregiving responsibilities. Another difficult transition is when adult children leave home to start their own lives. These life changes reduce our social interactions, leading to feelings of isolation and loneli-ness.

At times, I still feel lonely. So, what do I do? Have I learned anything in this area? I certainly sense the inner struggle when loneliness creeps in with those "poor me" or negative thoughts. But I've realized it's up to me to make a choice. I can either dwell on those feelings or turn to Jesus. And you know what? I choose Jesus! Whenever I feel lonely, I do what Jesus did—I try to reach out to others. I've found so much joy in lifting others up, making them laugh, sharing stories, and finding happiness daily. Overcoming loneliness continues to be a journey. I'm learning to choose not to stay in the "lonely zone" but to walk on with Jesus.

No matter where you are in life, whether caring for young children, having kids who are growing up and moving on, or experiencing a new kind of loneliness in the "empty nest" years, the wisdom in God's Word remains constant. James 1:2–3 (NIV) tells us, "Consider it pure joy, my brothers and sisters, whenever you face trials of many kinds, because you know that the testing of your faith produces perseverance." These verses are a powerful reminder that loneliness is intended to lead us to spiritual growth and strength.

We all experience loneliness at some point in our lives. The fact is, God walks with us every step of the way. We trust in Him and rely on Him to find pure joy in the life He places before us. C.S. Lewis once said, "Look for yourself, and you will find loneliness and despair. But look for Christ, and you will find Him and everything else." Just remember, we are never truly alone. If we trust Him wholeheartedly, Jesus Christ brings us into a deep and meaningful relationship. His love knows no bounds, and He is always there to guide, comfort, and support us through every step of our journey. Loneliness is a journey, not a destination.

About the Author

JUDY BONE IS A speaker, author, and seasoned Christian Image Consultant. She brings her unique Southern charm and humorous style to everything she does!

Drawing from her role as a minister's wife, Judy deeply understands women's trials and uses her "Let's Get Glowing" message to inspire audiences of all sizes. Judy radiates joy and encouragement when addressing large crowds, intimate gatherings, or engaging one-on-one.

Having battled and overcome esophageal cancer, Judy's narrative is not just about survival but about embracing life's laughter-filled moments and experiencing God's grace firsthand. Her book, *In His Glow,* is a testament to Judy's resilience and dedication, inspiring and motivating others with the transformative power of her faith in Christ.

As a seasoned Christian Image Consultant, Judy empowers women to discover their inherent beauty and cultivate confidence, regardless of age, body shape, or fashion preferences. Her expertise extends beyond appearances; she equips women with practical tools and enlightens them with spiritual insights to help them thrive daily.

Connect with Judy on her website at judybone.com
Email at flocklady@gmail.com
Facebook: Judy Bone
Instagram: @judybone
YouTube: @judybone177

CHAPTER 6

From Fixer to Faithful

A Story of Love, Loss, and Letting Go

As we played on the floor near my husband's recliner, our three-year-old granddaughter asked me, "Mimi, what will you do when Gampi dies?" Aby knew our family was facing a health crisis, and her curiosity deserved an honest answer.

Years ago, I would have assured her, "Oh Aby, I'll take such good care of Gampi; nothing bad will ever happen." I prided myself on being the person who meticulously orchestrated everything. That *was* me—the consummate fixer. But what happens when you are faced with an unsolvable challenge?

My husband's terminal brain cancer diagnosis, Glioblastoma Multiforme stage IV, showed me that no matter how hard I tried, I couldn't fix this. I wasn't in control. This reality check awakened a shift within me from being a fixer to a faithful follower of God. It wasn't an easy transition, but I have learned that grappling for control only deepened my struggle with self-reliance and pride. Releasing control and putting my trust in God allowed me to face any obstacle with the assurance that He is faithful.

The journey began on Saturday, July 10, 2004. I took my husband to our local emergency department for what we believed to be complications from a sinus infection. He had been on antibiotics for six weeks, but there was no improvement. When we walked into the hospital, neither of us anticipated that only thirty minutes later, he would be rushed to another hospital for emergency brain surgery. His CT scan revealed a brain tumor.

The biopsy report that came next had us in complete shock. It was cancer, and it was terminal. My first response was to fight; there must be something I could do. I became consumed with his treatment and care options. My world revolved around my husband's needs, and I took it upon myself to see he received the best possible care. There were days I felt like I was breathing for both of us. After all, we were married for over thirty years. What would I do without him? There must be something I could do; giving up was not an option. As I stood by his hospital bed, I came face-to-face with the reality that control is an illusion.

As caregivers, we often try to manage every aspect of the situation to ensure the best possible outcome. However, trying to hold everything together becomes too heavy to bear. I suddenly knew what Elisabeth Elliot meant when she said, "Fear arises when we imagine everything depends on us." I was carrying the weight of the world, and I needed to set it down and breathe.

As I faced losing my husband, I clung to Proverbs 3:5–6 (NIV). "Trust in the Lord with all your heart and lean not on your own understanding; in all your ways submit to him and he will make your paths straight." By surrendering control to God and acknowledging He is sovereign, I discovered His plans are greater than mine.

Christ's promise in John 14:27 (ESV) took on new meaning for me. "These things I have spoken to you while I am still with you. But the Helper, the Holy Spirit, whom the Father will send in my name, he will teach you all things and bring to your remembrance all that I have said to you. Peace I leave with you; my peace I give to you. Not as the world gives do I give to you. Let not your hearts be troubled, neither let them be afraid."

I began to understand that peace from God isn't just the absence of conflict or worry but the assurance that God is in control and that He sent a comforter and helper, the Holy Spirit. And His presence offered more help than I could ever provide. Once I stopped striving to control and fix everything, I discovered how to have an untroubled heart in a troubled world. The peace of God indeed does pass all understanding.

Accepting this shift was challenging, but it led me to focus on what I could do instead of what I couldn't do. The words of the apostle Paul remind us in 2 Corinthians 12:9 (NIV) that God's grace is sufficient, and His power is made perfect in our weakness. But the second half of that verse struck me most: "Therefore I will boast all the more gladly about my weaknesses, so that Christ's power may rest on me." Admitting my limitations and surrendering to God's control to work through my weaknesses gave me confidence in letting go, learning to lean on a power greater than my own, and finding peace despite a brain cancer diagnosis.

As we journeyed through the maze of cancer with its countless trips, scans, tests, chemotherapy, and radiation treatments, my husband insisted, "Jackie, we aren't dying of cancer. We are living with it."

I witnessed his determination, strength, and will to live, not just survive. There were also some funny moments along the way. The doctors compared my husband's brain surgery to "a file cabinet being dumped onto the floor." When my husband's "files" would go missing, when he'd forget something, he often joked that I must have put that bit of information in the wrong drawer.

Despite being given a six-month prognosis, my husband lived seven and a half years following his brain surgery. His positive attitude was a constant encouragement to me and others. The peace he demonstrated during his cancer journey gave me yet another example of God's love and care. This peace defies the world's definition.

Together, we celebrated not only seven years of living with brain cancer but also forty years of marriage. We aged together, like fine wine, learning what we truly loved and believed in—creating our own fresh bouquet. Staring a death sentence in the face and determining that every day is extraordinary helped us see the miracles surrounding us, and we learned to embrace each moment with gusto.

As my husband's health slowly deteriorated, we realized our journey together was about to change in a big way. During the sixteen months he was in hospice care in our home, we clung tightly to each other as we learned to put our trust in God's good design for our lives, even though that meant our days together would soon come to an end.

On April 13, 2012, my husband, Roy E. Freeman, died peacefully in my arms. God gave me the words needed in his final moments and the grace to let him go. As his heart raced and his breathing slowed, I said this to him:

"Babe, you are in the race of a lifetime. I see the finish line. When you cross over, you will be picked up like all the other victors. Your race will be won. You will turn and then begin to cheer me on because I will be right behind you. God has promised that. As the mist rises on our pond, and the birds start to sing, I see one lone star in the sky ... God will honor my wish. It will be okay for both of us. This I know! You will be with me everywhere. In every flower I plant, in the fragrance of each blossom, in every snowflake that falls, and in each wind that blows. You have left your mark, and it is good."

Though I am clinging to the peace of God, I continue to talk with Him about the many "whys" and "hows" of my life as I move forward without my husband. One thing is clear: caring for a spouse with terminal cancer requires letting go of control and accepting that God gives us what we need, not always what we want. I continue to hold fast to God's promise in Matthew 6:33 (NLT): "Seek the Kingdom of God above all else, and live righteously, and he will give you everything you need."

So, when my granddaughter asked, "Mimi, what will you do when Gampi dies?" I was able to give her the honest answer she deserved. Knowing that life and death are beyond my control, I said: "Aby, I will miss him terribly; I will talk about him every day and remember only the good things."

With her beautiful brown eyes, Aby looked up at me, smiled, and said, "That's good." Then, she returned to playing.

A child's simple question held profound meaning for me that day. I went from codependent to God-dependent and realized how to love and let go. I am eternally humbled and grateful God showed me I need to hold things and people of this world lightly, for they are temporal, and I need to hold tightly to His hand and His promises, for they are eternal.

Not everyone will face caring for a cancer patient, but each of us is on a journey of learning to surrender. When our circumstances are out of control, there is One who is in control. We can find hope in His Word and learn to relinquish everything to Him, trusting He will carry us to our finish lines. May the Lord carry you to yours.

About the Author

JACKIE FREEMAN IS AN author, speaker, and vocalist whose work spans across various genres and themes. Known for her heartfelt and insightful writing on grief, Jackie provides solace and understanding through her words to those navigating the difficult path of loss. She offers comfort and hope, drawing from her own experiences to connect deeply with her readers.

In addition to her tender reflections on grief, Jackie is also an accomplished children's book author. Her book *I'm Okay, Momma!* explores the fruit of the Spirit in a comforting and accessible way for young readers. *Bend Your Knees, Louise!* introduces children to the sport of pickleball, and quickly became an Amazon best-seller.

In the realm of devotionals, Jackie has penned *Unwrapping Christmas*, an Advent devotional that invites readers to discover the true spirit of the holiday season. *Keep a Song in Your Heart: Musical Notes for Daily Devotions* intertwines spiritual reflection with the power of music, each entry paired with a thoughtfully curated Spotify playlist.

Her most recent project, *A Journal for a JOYful Heart*, spans the four seasons, offering readers a space to reflect and find joy throughout the year. Each journal is also accompanied by a Spotify playlist, carefully selected to help quiet the mind and nurture the soul during each season of life.

As a speaker and vocalist, Jackie Freeman inspires audiences with her vibrant energy and passion through her stories, songs, and shared experiences. Whether through her books, speaking engagements, or music, Jackie's mission remains the same: to uplift, encourage, and bring a message of hope and joy.

Connect with Jackie:

Website: JackieFreemanAuthor.com
Email: jackie@jackiefreemanauthor.com
Instagram & Facebook: @jackiefreemanauthor

CHAPTER 7

Suffering and God's Silence

EACH NIGHT, I SAT on my bed praying, "God, please, no pain tonight. Please let us get some sleep. We are exhausted." Keeping my back straight, I'd maneuver myself into bed. My husband, Timmy, tucked pillows around me, trying to help me be more comfortable and experience less back and hip pain. Even if I got into a comfortable position, it was short-lived. When sleep finally found me, I'd wake up with my legs cramping and moving uncontrollably from restless leg syndrome (RLS), among other complications post-surgery.

Each sleepless night chiseled away at my faith. I had anticipated a spinal fusion surgery with confidence that God would be merciful with the pain and no complications would occur. Instead, God seemed merciless. Why didn't God intervene? Why didn't He send His comfort and grace? Was this my new normal? Had I made a mistake having this surgery where they drilled eighteen screws and two rods into my back?

My chronic pain started nine months before the surgery. A typical backache turned into sciatica one warm fall evening as I watered my yellow mums. A bolt of nerve pain shot down my leg and brought me to my knees. As sobs came, I could hear God telling me to rest. My days had been busy with preparations to publish my next book, so I agreed to rest one night. God had plans for more than rest. His plan included a significant break from my everyday life as a Christian writer and speaker.

We discovered that sciatica came from a severe case of scoliosis, but doctors didn't learn that for nearly half a year. Since I couldn't sit or stand without extreme pain, I spent most of my time in bed with ice packs. Do you remember the Tin Man on *The Wizard of Oz*? Each morning, I woke with every joint so stiff I felt like I needed the oil can to get moving.

Eventually, I saw a spine surgeon who started with epidurals, which helped immensely. I was able to walk again and return to church, but I still lived with great pain. Ultimately, I saw a specialist who corrects scoliosis with spinal fusion. He told me he needed to fuse ten vertebrae.

I endured the surgery, and life carried me from one level of pain to another. My mind felt like it was in a fog during recovery. I guess the effects of anesthesia and strong medications made it hard to think. I couldn't remember what I knew about having strong faith. I read the last book I wrote and wondered, "Who was this woman?"

I tried to stop questioning God and concentrated on physical therapy and walking. I walked laps in my driveway with my walker, trying to get stronger. For four months, I wore a heavy back brace whenever I was out of bed. Walking felt good, even though the summer heat made the brace wildly uncomfortable.

One summer afternoon, as I walked laps in the cool shade of my driveway, I realized the pain had stolen my hope, peace, and joy. Upon this realization, I stared ahead and determined to take them back from the enemy.

Regardless of my condition, I refused to allow the pain to steal my joy and peace. I knew where I had messed up. I took my eyes off Jesus.

As Peter walked on the water to Jesus, the stormy winds took his focus off his Lord. Peter began to sink. Before Peter yelled for Jesus to save him, he put his focus back on Jesus and put his faith back into action.

I had just written a book about having a faith that walks on water. I studied the story of Peter walking on water for several years while writing and speaking at churches, but I made the same mistake Peter made. My eyes focused on the pain and the deterioration of my life, making my health, or lack of it, my idol. Whatever we fixate on is our god, and when that isn't the one true God, it is an idol. I didn't idolize my pain. I didn't pray to my pain, but pain was front and center in my life.

As God showed me where I went wrong, He helped me return to the faith-filled woman I once was. I put my eyes back on Jesus. I took doubts captive and declared faith even when I didn't feel it. I began to give thanks and tried to quit complaining since Philippians 4:6–7 (NKJV) says, "Be anxious for nothing, but in everything by prayer and supplication, with thanksgiving, let your requests be made known to God; and the peace of God, which surpasses all understanding, will guard your hearts and minds through Christ Jesus."

Peace returned, as the above passage promises. I prayerfully reset my mind and fixed my eyes on Jesus. Now, I have hope once again. Scripture tells us to believe in the power of Jesus. We think that means all diseases will be healed and pain will have its limits.

Faith believes when God says yes, but faith grows when God says *no*. When God says to be patient, our faith grows.

Slowly, the pain inched away, and six months after surgery, I thought I would return to writing. Although my website traffic remained stable, my social media algorithms had forgotten who I was. Fatigued and depressed, I wondered, "What is the point of ministry?" I had lost my passion along with most of my followers, but a small, still voice kept whispering, "Don't stop."

I began attacking my depression, believing it was spiritual warfare. I'm not sure it wasn't, but in February 2024, my doctor changed my thyroid medication, and the depression lifted immediately. Finally, I felt like living again, even though some pain remained.

God encouraged me to return to our midweek church services. Yes, my back began hurting before I arrived; however, being with fellow believers lifted my spirits. The end of the day and sitting still create pain, but I keep my eyes on Jesus.

Next, I returned to the local flea market for a book signing, enduring four hours of sitting and standing.

Finally, God encouraged me to return to some of my speaker and writer online groups, and life felt normal again. Normal is good.

Friend, put your focus back on Christ during your crisis. Pain, whether emotional or physical, will block your view of Jesus. He will help you through and put people in your path to help you.

My husband became an excellent caregiver during this time. He went above and beyond, tending to my needs. Even though he worked from home during my recovery, he took time to help me walk every day. And each day, we walked a little further. I am blind and cannot walk without him or my guide dog. It was so disappointing not being able to walk my sweet Iva after surgery. When that day came, I celebrated it!

People think flowers and candy are the best gifts we can get from our spouses, but having someone walk you through the valley of death exceeds all gifts. Timmy demonstrated deep love, and our marriage is stronger for it.

Looking back at the most difficult journey of my life, I believe God carried me even though I felt I was alone. I still pray for healing in my nerves, but I can look back and see beauty where there were once ashes.

I've learned much about faith. It's not just believing God will deliver you from it but trusting God to carry you through it. Jesus, my Good Shepherd, comforted me with His rod and staff as He traveled with me through the valley of the shadow of death. I felt like a failure because my faith grew so shaky, but I know Jesus doesn't see me like that, and I hope I never have to traverse such a storm again. If I do, I hope to trust Him fully even when I can't see Him working.

I've also learned we must totally submit to God's ways and timetable rather than demanding our own ways through faith-filled declarations. Yes, God can heal, deliver, and make things happen sooner rather than later. I found strong faith trusts God to do things in His way and timing, not mine.

During the painful days after surgery, I kept seeing a vision of myself on stage speaking to a large audience. There were many days when it didn't seem possible, but I am already scheduled to speak again and have plans to procure more speaking engagements. I will share the message God has given me to encourage those who are suffering, especially in God's silence.

Perhaps that is you today, my friend. Again, I remind you to fix your eyes on Jesus, "looking unto Jesus, the author and finisher of *our* faith" (Hebrews 12:2, NKJV). Our faith begins with Jesus, and it ends with Him too. He consists of everything in between.

Pain and sickness are horrible places to go. Suffering demands our attention, robbing us of joy, peace, and hope. Hold onto joy because it isn't based on good circumstances. It is only based on Jesus.

Even in the most hopeless situations, Jesus remains our hope. Hang on, friend. He will bring you to the other side, just like He did with the disciples in the stormy sea and just as He did for me.

About the Author

CHRISTIAN SPEAKER AND AUTHOR **Carolyn Dale Newell** lives with blindness, but she calls her disability a gift from God. Her passion is equipping women to break free from emotional strongholds and live transformed lives. She has authored seven books, including her *Guide Dog Tales* devotional series and her new devotional journal with Redemption Press, *Faith That Walks on Water: Conquering Emotional Bondage with the Armor of God.*

Carolyn loves digging deep into Scripture and discovering truths she shares with her audience. She has earned a certificate in Biblical and Theological Foundations. She is a contributor for iBelieve.com and teaches Bible study at her home church. Carolyn is a member of the Advanced Writers and Speakers Association and a certified AWSA P.O.W.E.R. speaker. She has also earned speaker certifications through Activate with Mary R. Snyder and Speak Up with Carol Kent.

Carolyn resides in the Blue Ridge Mountains of Virginia with her husband, Tim. She loves reading, pizza, and discovering new independence with Iva, her guide dog.

Visit her website at amountainoffaith.com

CHAPTER 8

Autism, Actually

UNEXPECTED LESSON IN THE LOVE OF GOD

I WATCHED MY TYPICAL son disappear before my eyes, and I had to ask myself: Was I chasing the True Light or a false light? Am I persistently pursuing the light of our trustworthy God, all-powerful, all-knowing, eternal God, or the light of something else?

Time travel with me to 2006.

We had what appeared to be a picture-perfect dream of the typical social-me-dia-no-filter-needed family: a dad and a mom, two kids, a dog, and six cats. The number of cats might need a filter. Our daughter, whose first word was "hi," was rocking the local sports programs and was about to start preschool. Our son Thomas was walking and talking and loved solving puzzles, playing in the mud, and doing all the things a typical one-and-a-half-year-old boy would do. We sat in our not assigned but somehow same pew every week in church on Sundays and volunteered in all the places "good Christian families" volunteer. My purse even matched my shoes. We were the picture-perfect dream of a typical family. Until we weren't.

Thomas experienced typical development at first. He hit all his milestones. Crawling. Check. Walking. Check. Talking (dada, mama, truck). Checkity check. Then, at eighteen months, his language acquisition slowed. He seemed clumsier. He started to eat only certain foods. But at eighteen months, growth spurts and stops, spurts and stops. I knew this because of my vast knowledge of having one whole kid already and being a teacher by education and practice—I knew everyone grows at different, uneven rates. However, at two years old, Thomas didn't just slow down in his word acquisition; he stopped gaining new words altogether.

At his next pediatrician appointment, I voiced my concerns about Thomas's language and motor skills slowing down. The doctor did not seem overly concerned. He assured me there would be an explosion of language in the next six months.

"An Explosion of Language." I can still see those words hanging over the pediatrician's head in one of those cartoon speech bubbles. Instead of the explosion of language, over the next six months, Thomas's words disappeared one by one. Our beautiful, smiley, snuggly son drifted away and completely withdrew into a secret place inside himself.

His typical love of crashing his toy cars and trucks together was exchanged for lining them up into rows. His typical love of being read to was exchanged for staring blankly at the cover of a book as if he couldn't remember how to open it. His typical smile was replaced with averted eye contact. His eyes ... his clear blue eyes ... were vacant.

We scheduled Thomas for an evaluation. It was a month and a half before Thomas's third birthday. In my heart of hearts, I hoped I wouldn't hear what the doctor said as I sat across a desk from her the first week of December 2007.

"Your son has autism."

In an instant that had taken months to arrive, my picture-perfect dream of a typical social-media-no-filter-needed family—a dad and a mom, two kids, a dog, and six cats (yes, still six cats)—transformed into something unexpected and unplanned: an autism diagnosis.

I gave the outward appearance of Christian success. I had a checklist of the picture-perfect typical Christian family, and it had been working for me. Church attendance. Check. Bible study. Check. Volunteering. Check. Being nice to people. Mostly check. Now, the outward appearance of Christian success that I valued offered me no comfort. I felt adrift and abandoned and alone.

For the better part of a year, I hid my fears and feelings from God and others. Oh, I was still showing up in church and Bible study because I didn't want people to know I didn't have my stuff together. However, in my heart, I was hiding from the all-powerful, all-knowing, eternal God.

Clearly, I'm a genius.

One of the places I showed up was a Bible study of the book of Romans. I loved the study of Romans because, as a long-time church girl, the story was familiar to me. It lays out the gospel of Jesus Christ. It explains our salvation in Him, but it also kicked me in the teeth in a very unexpected way when I needed it most. The Romans study helped me put together some of the pieces of the life I once dreamed of but no longer had. I learned more about God's heart and how He sees me, sees Thomas, and sees all of us. We are His creation, and He doesn't make mistakes—He apparently leaves those to us. Here are some more things I learned.

"For all have sinned and fall short of the glory of God" Romans 3:23 (ESV).

Yeah, they have! I mean … yes, I have.

"But God shows his love for us in that while we were still sinners, Christ died for us" Romans 5:8 (ESV).

God demonstrated His love for us. Not after we got our stuff together. *While* we were sinners.

"For the wages of sin is death, but the free gift of God is eternal life in Christ Jesus our Lord" Romans 6:23 (ESV).

We receive eternal life as a gift by choosing to accept Jesus Christ as our savior. He paid the price for our sins. We are saved by grace alone through faith in Christ alone. Yes, and amen! All of those things. Those were familiar promises to me. That was the trustworthy God I knew. That's hope!

But in the middle of that Romans thread, I read this: "Not only that, but we rejoice in our sufferings, knowing that suffering produces endurance, and endurance produces character, and character produces hope, and hope does not put us to shame, because God's love has been poured into our hearts through the Holy Spirit who has been given to us" (Romans 5:3–5 ESV).

Rejoice in our sufferings? That seemed dumb.

But the hope? The hope that does not put us to shame? The NASB uses the phrase "hope that does not disappoint." As ridiculous as "rejoicing in suffering" sounded, the "hope that didn't disappoint"—I needed that badly.

Romans 8 broke me open. "For I am convinced that neither death nor life, neither angels nor demons, neither the present nor the future, nor any powers, neither height nor depth, nor anything else in all creation, will be able to separate us from the love of God that is in Christ Jesus our Lord" (Romans 8:38–39, NIV).

As I read those words, I cried—an ugly, snotty nose with red, puffy eyes sobbing until you can't breathe cry—because I did feel separated from the love of God.

I felt separated from God and other people because my life wasn't typical. My life wasn't like everyone else's. At the beginning of Thomas's autism diagnosis, his social and emotional differences weren't as pronounced, but as my friends' children grew in skill, Thomas seemed to regress. And I can say this now but couldn't at the time; I was embarrassed. As if his behavior, or lack thereof, was a parenting failure. I started to believe the lies that the devil was whispering in my ear:

- Everyone is looking at you.

- Everyone is judging you.

- No good can come from this autism diagnosis.

Surrounded by walls of pain and shame, I let the devil get me alone to fill my mind and heart with the lies that my children and I were not worthy of someone's effort to be seen. I hid behind my carefully constructed facade, thinking that everything would be fine for a long time. I thought I was protecting my family and myself. I didn't feel like we "fit in" or really that I "fit in," which is a lie I have struggled with my whole life.

I watched my typical son disappear before my eyes, and I had to ask myself: Was I chasing the True Light or a false light? Was I persistently pursuing the light of God, all-powerful, all-knowing, eternal, or the light of something else? Perhaps the light of some typical picture-perfect Christian life?

However, Romans 8:38 and 39 promised me that this nontypical, neurodivergent life was not going to separate me from God's love. It wouldn't separate Thomas from God's love. The love of God is not conditional. We don't have to earn it. We *can't* earn it. It's a gift of God, not based on our abilities. That was the hope that didn't disappoint. That's the hope I needed, the promise I could cling to.

The love of God is atypical.

When I stopped focusing on my picture-perfect dream of the typical social-media-no-filter-needed family and started focusing on the atypical love of God, a transformation started in my heart. Having a son on the autism spectrum brought to the surface some wrong attitudes I was carrying around in my purse that matched my shoes.

I was an ultracompetitive firstborn with control issues and a deep, ugly, judgmental streak. Then, I had a child who didn't learn at the same rate as his peers or respond quickly to questions. His speech is hard to understand. Thomas stims and hums and squeals when we're out and about. Stim is short for stimulating behaviors that soothe you when you're anxious. You might tap your foot or twist your hair. Those are stims. We have a saying in our house now: We all have special needs. Some of us are just better at hiding them.

Thomas has only told me, "I love you," unprompted one time. He doesn't do too many things to intentionally earn my love. I mean, we don't expect people to earn our love, do we? Yet, I love Thomas endlessly.

Do you know who else loves Thomas endlessly? Do you know who loves you endlessly? I'll give you a hint: reread Romans 8:38–39. Thomas' atypical, neuro-divergent behaviors no longer cause me to feel adrift, alone, and abandoned. Wait. That's not true. My feelings of being adrift, alone, and abandoned by Thomas's atypical, neurodivergent behaviors continue to decrease the more I focus on God and not the behaviors.

Having a son on the autism spectrum has created compassion on a whole new level. Although I would not wish an autism diagnosis on anyone, frankly, I don't know that I would have learned this level of compassion any other way. I continue the pursuit of replacing my typical, ultracompetitive firstborn with control issues and a deep, ugly, judgmental streak tendencies with the atypical love of God. How did that happen? Well, it was and continues to be a process. The first step involved taking small, intentional steps toward God. And when I say small, I mean small.

A wise mentor mom saw how much I was struggling and asked how I was doing. In an uncharacteristically honest moment, I admitted life was not kittens and rainbows. She listened intently as I unleashed the emotional tsunami that was my fears of being adrift, alone, and abandoned. She kept smiling and nodding kindly. She was fully present with me at that moment. I didn't realize how much isolation had robbed me until she broke through my facade of the picture-perfect dream of a typical family.

When I was finished with my verbal vomit, she asked how my time with God was going. My answer must have been written on my face because even though I was silent, she made this suggestion: one verse. Three index cards. One month. She encouraged me to write one verse on three index cards and put them in three places where I found myself daily. For one month, I was to read that same verse every time I saw it on the card. This seemed too small a task. I told her I thought I could do one verse a week.

Her gentle but direct response still rings true all these years later. "It's not about what you can do. It's about what God will do."

And she was right. Reading those verses for a month as I was at the kitchen sink (dishes!), in the car (so many therapy appointments), and in the bathroom (sometimes Mama needs a time out) pierced my hard heart and over time developed into a habit of daily Bible time with God. Small, intentional steps. With every step I took toward the atypical love of God, my fears of being adrift, alone, and abandoned transformed into feelings of being secure, seen, and saved. That was a light worth pursuing. That *is* a light worth pursuing.

If you feel less than or atypical, remember you are made in the image of God. The first chapter of the first book of the Bible tells us, "So God created man in his own image, in the image of God he created him; male and female he created them" (Genesis 1:27, ESV). God never changes. He's still in the business of creating His people in His image. Zephaniah 3:17 (ESV) tells us, "The Lord your God is in your midst, a mighty one who will save; he will rejoice over you with gladness; he will quiet you by his love; he will exult over you with loud singing." He rejoices and exults over us! Imagine God rejoicing and exulting over you. He does ... because He made you. He's excited about *you.*

About the Author

WELCOME **LaCINDA HALLS**. SHE loves vegetable gardening, watching British television shows, and sharing her love of the Bible with people of all ages. The love of God is for all His children, no exceptions! This truth continues to grow clearer to her as she loves and cares for Thomas, their nonverbal son on the autism spectrum who can pass gas on demand.

With twenty-five years of teaching experience, LaCinda offers hope, humor, and Jesus to women who need assurance that our stories have a purpose in His plan and that nothing can separate us from the love of God.

You can connect with LaCinda:

Website: lacindahalls.com
Faceboook: @lacindahalls
Instagram: @lacindahalls

CHAPTER 9

The Stranger on the Corner

HOW A HOMELESS MAN CHANGED MY HEART

FOR WEEKS, AS I walked from the bus to my office, I passed a young man sitting at a corner with his hand outstretched, an old coffee cup at his feet, and a sign that read "HUNGRY." Each morning, he greeted me with a "good morning," but I walked by him without making eye contact or uttering a single word. Despite my silence, I felt a pang of guilt each time I ignored him.

One day, I resolved to change the way I was behaving. The next morning, I directed my steps toward him, stopped by his side, and said, "Good morning. How are you doing today?" while dropping money into his cup. The young man jumped up, looked me in the eye, and said, "You are the first person to say good morning." Shame washed over me as I hung my head, muttered an excuse, and continued walking to work.

The following day, he was waiting for me. As I approached, he stood up, and we exchanged a few words before I, once again, cut our conversation short to head to work. I felt unsettled and guilty for not doing more or engaging with him longer. Determined to change that, I left for work earlier the next day so I could talk with him for longer and find out his name and where he came from.

With a lighter step and a smile, I approached his corner, excited to talk with him. But he was gone. I searched the street, walking a block in each direction, but he was nowhere to be found. Disappointed, I went to work, hoping to see him the next day. I approached the corner for a week, hoping to find him, but he never reappeared. I asked around, determined to find him, but no one knew who I was referring to. To this day, when I approach that corner, memories of him come flooding back.

Though I may not know what happened to him, he taught me an invaluable lesson: to acknowledge everyone. Now, I keep change handy, greet those who approach me on the street or knock on my car window with a smile, and say "hello" and "have a good day." I have learned to see society's invisible. I don't know what drives them to the streets or their stories, but I want them to know they are seen.

Reflecting on this experience, I am reminded of the biblical command to love and acknowledge our neighbors. In Matthew 25:35–40 (NIV), Jesus says, "For I was hungry, and you gave me something to eat, I was thirsty and you gave me something to drink, I was a stranger, and you invited me in, [...] The King will reply, 'Truly I tell you, whatever you did for one of the least of these brothers and sisters of mine, you did for me.'" This young man was a stranger to me, yet I was fulfilling a divine mandate in acknowledging him.

Proverbs 19:17 (NIV) teaches us that "Whoever is kind to the poor lends to the Lord, and he will reward them for what they have done." Every small act of kindness, every moment of recognition, is a gift to those in need and a service to God.

This experience has opened my eyes to several important truths:

The Power of Presence

First and foremost, acknowledging someone's presence is a powerful act. In our fast-paced world, it's easy to overlook those around us, especially those who might seem different or are in difficult situations. By saying "good morning," I offered a small piece of humanity and dignity to someone who felt invisible. This small act of presence is incredibly powerful, reminding us that everyone deserves to be seen and heard.

Breaking Down Barriers

Interacting with the young man broke down barriers in my own heart. Initially, I felt uncomfortable and out of my comfort zone. But as I tried to engage with him, I began to see him not just as a homeless person but as a fellow human being with his own story and struggles. This shift in perspective is crucial in our walk of faith. Jesus broke down barriers, reaching out to those marginalized and forgotten by society. In John 4, Jesus speaks with the Samaritan woman at the well, breaking social and cultural norms to show her compassion and understanding. By following His example, we, too, can break down the barriers that separate us from others.

Reflecting God's Love

Our interactions with others are an opportunity to reflect God's love. In 1 John 4:19 (NIV), we read, "We love because he first loved us." This means that our capacity to love others comes from the love we receive from God. When we show kindness and compassion to those in need, we reflect the love God has shown us. This not only brings comfort to those we help but also deepens our relationship with God. It's a way of living out our faith in a tangible, impactful way.

The Ripple Effect

Acts of kindness, no matter how small, create a ripple effect. By taking the time to acknowledge the young man, I was not only impacting his life but also changing my heart and potentially inspiring others to do the same. In Galatians 6:9, Paul encourages us, "Let us not become weary in doing good, for at the proper time we will reap a harvest if we do not give up." Our consistent efforts to do good, even in small ways, lead to greater change and a harvest of kindness and compassion in our communities.

The Call to Action

This experience is a call to action for all of us. We are surrounded by people who may feel invisible or overlooked. By making a conscious effort to acknowledge and show kindness to others, we are living out the teachings of Christ. James 2:14–17 reminds us that faith without deeds is dead. Our faith should compel us to act, to reach out, and to make a difference in the lives of others.

What I learned from this young man is profound and life-changing. By acknowledging the invisible, breaking down barriers, reflecting God's love, understanding the ripple effect of kindness, and answering the call to action, we can live out our faith in meaningful and impactful ways. Though he may never know it, this young man taught me one of my life's greatest lessons. Through him, I learned to see, to care, and to love more deeply. And for that, I am forever grateful. Overcoming my discomfort in approaching someone different has made a significant difference in how I relate to others, fostering a deeper sense of empathy and connection.

I encourage you to do the same. Step out of your comfort zone, acknowledge those around you, and let your actions be a testament to the love and compassion we are called to show.

About the Author

RUTH HOVSEPIAN IS A speaker, author, and podcast host who shares her powerful journey of addiction and sobriety to inspire and support others facing similar challenges.

Ruth endured an acrimonious separation and divorce when her three children were young—her youngest was just five months old. As a single mother, she faced the daunting task of providing for her family, returning to school, and building a successful career in IT. Despite climbing to the top of her field, Ruth struggled with a double life: a dedicated mother and businesswoman by day and a "party girl" by night. Reflecting on those years, she recognizes the dangerous and life-threatening path she once walked.

With nine years of sobriety behind her, Ruth has found a renewed sense of purpose and a deepened relationship with God. She published her first book, *100 Days of Prayer: A Journey into Deeper Intimacy with God*, in 2022. Her latest book, *A Mother's Love*, was released in the spring of 2024. Through her writing and speaking, Ruth empowers others to find joy, hope, healing, and purpose, encouraging them to write their own stories of transformation.

Other books that Ruth has authored:

The Ultimate Conversation: Is that you, GOD? (Bible Study)
Prepare Him Room: 25 Devotions Celebrating the Birth of Jesus
Praying the Promises of the Cross: 40-day devotional journal

Ruth also hosts *Out of the Darkness with Ruth Hovsepian,* a podcast that explores faith, transformation, and finding light in the darkest moments.

Connect with Ruth:

Podcast: Out of the Darkness with Ruth Hovsepian
Instagram: @ruthhovsepian
Facebook: @ModernDayRuthRedeemed
Website: ruthhovsepian.com

CHAPTER 10

The Woman at the Well

How many of us have been invited to the well? But are we thirsty enough to go? I want to take you on the journey of my well.

As I traveled to my well that day, all alone, not seeing any other way out from all the destruction I caused, I found myself in the middle of the floor with a gun in my hand to end it all. But then I heard God's voice speaking very clearly, "No, not now. Now you are at a place I can heal you."

Right in the heat of the day at my well, God promised healing—healing from the broken life I was living—healing from the destructive life I created. It took four decades to build the tangled web of ruin I called my life.

When did this wreckage start? It started as a child. It started with someone else's decision to abuse me sexually, which began a spiral into a self-imposed prison. I locked myself away, grasping tightly to those prison bars, and started the journey down a road of pure destruction.

I became a mother at sixteen years old. The enemy's lies told me I was damaged goods and that I would never be good enough for anyone to *really* love. Believing his lies, I found alcohol and liked it way more than I should have. It became my companion, and like many relationships, it started slowly, but it became my number one friend as I looked for the many answers I longed for at the bottom of the bottle.

I found myself between my second and third marriage, and again, the lies were winning. I was homeless with two beautiful little girls, finding shelter in my truck until my brother offered us his dining room. Everything we owned fit into a few small piles. I was thankful for the safety of that small room.

Fast forward, and my fourth marriage was headed to divorce court. I was so tired of the fights, lies, and the feeling I would never be good enough. I just wanted a way out to end all the misery and shame. And that's when God reached down and said He would heal me.

At that moment, I could feel the chains start falling off the doors of the prison cell I'd locked myself in. The chains didn't magically fall off as if I were Wonder Woman, whose links immediately broke off when she threw her arms out. God showed me things that had to be done—one link at a time.

The next steps were some of the hardest I have ever taken. I told my husband and family the ugly truth about all the abusive years. Then, I had to choose forgiveness. I had to choose to forgive the one who had started this runaway freight train many years ago. The choices he made to abuse me were his, but the road of destruction and choices I made were mine, and I had to own them. I had to own the other titles I wore: adulterer, liar, and thief.

While the one who robbed my childhood had passed long ago, I still had to face him. I chose to face him as I imagined him sitting in the empty chair before me. All the anger, hatred, and unforgiveness came out while I cried more tears than I ever thought one person could shed. Deliverance was coming, and with it, a promise of healing. Over the next four years, God brought me through a process of revealing chain links breaking; those chain links came in the form of things I had taken hold of but needed to release to receive the freedom to move forward.

During my four-year journey, I repeated Psalm 139:23–24 (NIV) over and over. "Search me, God, and know my heart; test me and know my anxious thoughts. See if there is any offensive way in me, and lead me in the way everlasting." I knew if I was going to receive His healing, I needed to be shown what things were and were not of Him, and I needed His guidance through them.

The journey of healing was fulfilled one day with a word from the Lord. "Now it is done." God promised me healing, and He delivered. From that day on, He's led me on a path that only the Good Father, our Creator, could construct. He's been faithful to His word, has taken me on adventures, and led me to places and people who have blessed my heart more than I can measure.

Many times, I stand and argue with Him about giving my testimony. After all, who signs up to share the messy parts of their lives with others? No one is looking for more judgment or negativity spoken against them. But God constantly reminds me that it's not my story to tell. It's His story. It's the history of Jesus Christ. It's about the miracles He did in the lives of the people over two thousand years ago when He walked in the flesh. And it's what He did in my life and what He will do in your life.

God loves us in the mess just as much as He loves us when He's cleaned us up. No one's life is beyond redemption. God sent His Son to save the very people He has created. Allow God to rewrite your story and become His story.

I have been told repeatedly that I should not share my dark story—that it gives the enemy glory. But that is nothing more than a lie from the pits of Hades. We give the enemy glory when we keep holding onto the darkness. Step out, break the cycle, and share your story. Let the light that the Father has instilled in you become a beacon for others.

There is an old quote, and I'm not sure who wrote it, but a precious sister inside the prison units gave it to me. "The ones who come to Jesus and know they have been forgiven have no problem talking about their past; the ones on the fence still try to hide their past."

Be a fence breaker.

I'm no longer ashamed to share my story. The old titles are gone. I carry new ones now. I am a daughter, sister, wife, mother, grandmother, minister, ministry leader, and business owner. I am proud of each of these titles. But the title I am most proud of is the one that He has given me. I am a daughter of the Most High King, and He is not done with me yet.

He has given me a voice for the ones who can't speak for themselves, a love for the ones everyone else wants to throw away, and a compassion for women who think they will never be worthy of love. As our Father will never waste anything, He met me at my well and filled me with living water. And now, I share inside prison walls, on the streets, and on stages large and small, because my story is His story.

I depend on these two Bible verses:

> But you will receive power when the Holy Spirit comes on you; and you will be my witnesses in Jerusalem, and in all Judea and Samaria, and to the ends of the earth.
>
> Acts 1:8 (NIV)

> Therefore, if anyone is in Christ, the new creation has come: The old has gone, the new is here!
>
> 2 Corinthians 5:17 (NIV)

I became new in Jesus Christ, and you can too. Together, let's find renewed hope and make our stories His stories.

About the Author

SANDRA JONES IS THE founder of Homeless Heart Ministry. For over a decade, she has brought a message of encouragement, hope, and love to audiences of all sizes. She ministers to women in the areas of identity, forgiveness, and freedom from the difficulties life has dealt them. She believes when we grasp the depth of love our Savior has for us, we will leave the past behind and move forward, knowing the joy of the Lord is our strength.

As a Bible teacher and women's and prison ministry leader, she would love to share a fresh way for your audience to experience God like never before.

Sandra and her husband, Jackie, have three children, six grandchildren, and one fur baby that rules their household. They have enjoyed renovating and living in a 100-year-old church for nearly half a decade, and God has them on the move again to the heart of East Texas.

Sandra loves to share with women about who they truly are in God's eyes, and she loves to hear from her readers and contacts. If you want more information on booking Sandra, contact her at sandrajonesspeaks@gmail.com or her website sandrajonesspeaks.com.

CHAPTER 11

Where Misery and Miracles Meet

"It's not supposed to be *this* hard," I thought as I pulled the cheap plastic pen from the cup and scratched my name onto the next available line of the patient sign-in sheet. The receptionist must have spoken to me because the words "Good morning! How are you today?" seemed to be floating in the space just behind my head, not quite making it to the inside just yet. I knew I had to reply. I also knew if I said anything other than, "I'm fine, how are you?" this poor woman would know exactly how not-fine I really was, so that's exactly what came out of my mouth. "I'm fine. How are you?"

My eyes never met hers, but somehow, she felt the ache I was masking deep in my soul because she instantly said, "Oh no, you're not ... what's wrong?"

When our eyes finally met, the first soldier of my army of tears hit the stark paper below me with a splat, smearing the fresh ink. Immediately, the sweet receptionist, who got much more than she bargained for, asked if I needed a hug. I was gutted. Sobbing at the front desk of the chiropractor's office that Friday morning was definitely not on my to-do list, but here I was, offering a front-row seat to my messy life.

As I made my way back to a therapy bed, I hurriedly wiped the tears off hot cheeks as my nose continued its drippy symphony. Staring at the sterile ceiling, I tried to avoid the overly bright lights as the roller in the bed moved up and down the length of my spine. I was a mess—physically, mentally, emotionally ... all the "-allys." You know, like when you pick up your phone to snap a pic and realize how greasy you must be because the lens is covered in fingerprints, and you can't see a darn thing. That's how I felt at that moment.

How did I get here?

We were in a hard season with a sick kiddo in need of surgery who wasn't sleeping, which means I wasn't sleeping either. That couldn't be it, right? I know sleep deprivation is literal torture, but that couldn't be all that was wrong with me. I survived back-to-back newborn stages with babies who refused to sleep. Surely, I could survive an extended period of sickness.

Spoiler alert ... I couldn't.

Crying into the arms of a stranger should have been my first clue, but I really like to make God work when He is trying to get through to me.

The absolute last place I pictured myself as we neared the end of a decade-long infertility journey was as a stay-at-home homeschool mom to three adopted miracles. We exhausted every effort to start a family on our own volition. Every single one. Our final attempt at creating a family was thwarted on a Thursday in May. We had been walking out the potential of a surrogate option to grow our family, and one "no" prevented us from moving forward in the process. When the doctor told me that the one thing we didn't feel comfortable doing was the only way it could happen, I knew my chances of being a mother were over ... But God. Three days later, on Sunday, I discovered my son existed. Oh, and not just any Sunday. It was Mother's Day!

From our first meeting to holding him in our arms as our own, God gave this former control freak a whopping forty-eight hours to prepare for the most life-altering change. Hi, my name is Lindsay, and it's true: I used to be a horrible control freak until God started hand-delivering me children over and over and over again. He didn't redeem our infertility with just one miracle; He gave us three miracles.

When He hand-delivered our second baby, it was a snowy Christmas Eve, and from phone call to hospital pick-up, we had a full four hours and thirty-seven minutes to prepare. Then again, eleven months later, a similar phone call and twenty-four hours later, another beautiful tiny baby girl joined our family. We were not trained foster parents awaiting our first foster child or working with a pricey agency, awaiting our birth mother match moment. God quite literally nudged people in our direction who made connections on our behalf, completely unsolicited.

When I say God delivered, He *delivered*!

Life was chaos, but it was our beautiful chaos. Adoptions are hard and wonderful, a full tug-of-war between fear and faith. You worry about everything, and the battle doesn't end at the bang of a gavel. If anything, that's when it begins.

I genuinely felt that after our hard-fought battle, I would feel free from the isolating pressures of the adoption process. I would no longer feel like I was being weighed and measured by caseworkers and social workers and magistrates. I would no longer have to prove myself worthy of parenting these children that I was so miraculously gifted, and I could share a photo of them without covering their sweet little faces with an emoji.

To my dismay, it's not what happened. I found myself deep in the throes of mothering two toddlers simultaneously. I floundered at best, but it looked like I had it all together. Oh man, I hate that phrase. Literally, no one "has it all together," so can we stop saying this, please?

I had the three miracle babies, the backyard brimming with all the kid things, the pantry full of snacks, and the playroom full of toys. Anyone who entered my home could easily see the goodness of God. After a decade-long drought,

God delivered the rain! But along with the rain came all the other things. Sticky handprints on every window, door, and mirror. Crumbs on every surface at every moment, even when I just vacuumed the floors and wiped down the counters. Unending piles of laundry. Clutter and chaos on every surface. Abandoned Legos that left a permanent indentation on your foot when you accidentally stepped on them.

We had evidence of God's goodness all around us, even in our disarray. However, I found myself craving time away. Time to "just be me." It felt like I was continuously running a marathon in slippers—for seven years. I was exhausted and most definitely in the wrong shoes. I had nothing left. I thought if I could just get away and allow myself a much-needed reset, then I'd be okay. I could keep up the pace and be fine.

When God hand-delivered my three miracles, I must have misinterpreted His call on my life, right? I must have heard Him say: "Here, sweet girl. Your infertility battle is won. Here are your miracles. Care for them well. Love them. Sacrifice all of who you are for them. Never take care of yourself. You are not the priority; they are. I'm leaving this solely up to you now. My work is done. You can do this on your own. Don't screw it up, okay?"

That's absolutely not the God I know. I put all that nonsense on myself. I made myself too available. Nothing was off limits. There were no boundaries. If God gave me these miracles, I would never stop making sure they had what they needed. I did the best, used the best, was the best. I worked my butt off, but the only place you couldn't tell I'd been working so hard was my actual butt.

A subconscious resentment snuck into my heart. With every meal planned, prepared, and cleaned up, I ensured the kids were fed, but rarely myself. With every load of laundry washed, dried, and folded, I ensured the kids had all they could ever need, but my clothes were never clean and began to look dingy. By midafternoon, the sound of my new moniker "mom" began to sound more like a dentist's drill than the melodious miracle it actually was. I found myself full of bitterness and resentment, but I genuinely had no idea why. Surely, it wasn't my children; they are miracles straight from heaven. So why was this so hard for me?

Was it this hard for everyone, but no one really talked about it? I assumed my thoughts were true and continued to chug along.

Never getting respite.

Never caring for myself.

Never taking a break.

I broke my body to the point of three heel spurs, plantar fasciitis, Achilles tendonitis, and bursitis, and that's just my feet. When I say I broke myself, I physically broke myself.

I cared for them without caring for me even a little. This was my choice, but Satan tempted me to blame them internally. If I was hungry, it was the kids' fault. If I hadn't showered in days, it was the kids' fault. I blamed them for everything, never sharing with anyone how I was really feeling. My subconscious emotional blame spiral led me to feel the need to zone out, to be distracted from my feelings. I found myself using the bathroom as a break room, leaving the kids in front of the TV with a snack so I could take five minutes, sit down for the first time, get on my phone to play mindless games and scroll the flawless motherhood of others on social media, further perpetuating my issues.

I hid all of this from everyone, too afraid to see their reactions. The one time I told a friend that I thought I was too available for my children, she looked at me like I was growing a unicorn horn. Naturally, I didn't feel inclined to share my feelings with anyone else for fear a rainbow mane would follow the sparkling horn.

I started to question my entire life. After crying at the chiropractor's office, I knew something had to change. I was low. I thought about what would happen if I just left. Maybe it would be better for everyone. I began overusing pain medication just to make it through the day and then as a reward when I did.

If I'm being fully transparent, I'm not completely through this season in my life. I'm still in the thick of toddler tantrums and learning how to care for myself, but God has shown me something so powerful I must share with you. I heard someone say, "Satan hates children," and I couldn't get it out of my mind. It repeated on a loop, like the hook of a summertime one-hit wonder. Then it hit me. Satan hates children ... including my own. Could these issues be something more than my kids being tough and me being a boundaryless mom who is far too available for her children?

It's always something more, isn't it?

This case was no different. Satan was manipulating my miracles, using them against me to keep me from my call in Christ. I am called to care for them, but I couldn't do that if I was full of bitterness and resentment.

During this season of unraveling and discovering, I began naturally waking up much earlier than normal, despite my habit of staying up far too late in an attempt to garner some precious alone time. It must be the sun, I thought. We don't have blackout curtains, and I made it my goal to remedy that, stat. I researched curtains, scouring the best of Amazon and Target, but I couldn't pull the trigger. Also, very unlike me—I'm an instant gratification kind of girl. I sat with the thought of buying blackout curtains for almost a week, blaming my indecision on the kids' continual interruptions preventing me from ordering.

Then I heard the whisper that only He can give. "Instead of buying curtains, get up and meet with Me." I thought, "That sounds nice, but God, I already don't sleep enough. Can You not take this one thing from me?" Then it hit me. My reaction was quite the opposite of what I would hope to receive from my own children. Talk about perspective. "Okay, Lord, I'll get up and meet with You when You wake me up."

And I did.

Some days, it was fifteen minutes before the kids woke up. Some days, it was two hours before the kids woke up. Yet with each block of time He carved out, I grabbed my Bible and my version of coffee and connected with Him. The camera smudges slowly began to clear, and I realized I had never told anyone how desperate my thought life had become. No one knew how deep my bitterness and resentment ran, and looking from the outside, you'd never know it. I was praised by those around me for my patience and how I handled my children when they demonstrated poor behavior. I may have handled it well on the outside, but inside, it was another story. When I realized how different my insides felt versus how my outsides appeared, I knew I couldn't keep up the charade much longer.

I finally processed my feelings and surrendered them to the Lord. After meeting with Him daily and really doing the work to journal my feelings, I was ready to confess. I knew the only way through these feelings was to admit I had them in the first place.

Confession is an act so often associated with Catholic priests listening intently behind a shadowy screen, not something everyone is accustomed to, especially someone like me who wasn't raised in Catholicism. In our family, we could talk about our problems, but I was taught to be proper, and confessing my sins seemed anything but proper. I was comfortable confessing only to God. That felt safe enough at the beginning of my adult Christian walk because I was one who would never purposefully reach the point of discomfort.

I attended a worship night once where a ten-year-old performed a rap song he wrote. One of the lines at the beginning revealed he was the product of his mother selling her body to a stranger in exchange for drug money and how she was going to get an abortion. However, she decided to walk out of the clinic just before they started the procedure. He made it very clear that he is only here today because of God's faithfulness. I was undone in the best way. He was so young, and his message was so profound. After his performance, the announcer shared that his mama was in the audience and encouraged her to take the stage. She did so and immediately confessed her story of addiction and prostitution ... but God. This eye-opening testimony showed me that confession isn't just an upward conversation. We must confess to those around us. It not only frees us from the bondage of our sin, but it allows those around us to receive the testimony of God's goodness.

Psalm 34:5 (CSB) says, "Those who look to him are radiant with joy; their faces will never be ashamed." We are not meant to live in the bondage of sin and shame. When I shared what I was going through with my people, most of them were shocked but immediately receptive to my story. They stood beside me and assured me I had done the right thing by telling them. I received prayers that could never have been raised had I not confessed. The fog began to lift, and I started to see more clearly the goodness of God through the blur of the enemy's manipulation. I leaned into the Spirit and confessed all the things. I began telling more and more people about what I realized about Satan, and I knew this was a story that wasn't done being written.

As I continue to surrender my need for control and confess my sins by sharing my story, I can spot more clearly when my mindset begins wandering into dangerous territory. When the sound of my miracles makes me grimace on the inside, when I start to think solely of my own sacrifices for our family, when something insignificant they do sets me off, I feel that Spirit nudge saying, "It's time to confess and surrender again." When I follow His lead, my kids feel like miracles once again.

My life is still far beyond my control, but these days, I'm absolutely content giving my worries and need for control to my Father, knowing full well His shoulders are broad enough to carry my burdens.

What burdens do you carry today?

Now think back for a second. Were these burdens once your miracles?

I encourage you to spend time with the Lord. I know you feel like you don't have any extra time to spare. I did too. If this is you, the answer is simple. Just tell Him to wake you up when He wants to meet with you, and when He does, get out of bed, sis, and sit with Him. Lap in the luxury of alone time with the King of Kings. Surrender your burdens to Him, for He wants to help you carry them.

In Matthew 11:28–30, Jesus invites us to give Him our burdens. Surrender the tough things, the heaviness weighing you down, and allow Him to turn your burdens back into the miracles they once were. The time you are so worried about not having enough of right now will begin to turn into the time you cherish more than any other minute of the day.

Last, share with others. Confession is often an unknown blessing. James 5:16 (NIV) says, "Therefore confess your sins to each other and pray for each other so that you may be healed. The prayer of a righteous person is powerful and effective." Had I never confessed my sinful thought life, I could have missed the blessings my prayer warriors provided. Don't miss it. Don't miss the best God has for you. I promise you, it's worth it. You are worth it!

About the Author

LINDSAY TEDDER IS AN author and comedic storyteller who absolutely refuses to turn her light off for anyone or anything! She will ensure you keep your light shining bright as well. After ten (ten!) whole years of infertility and at the lowest low of her life, God showed up in a *big* way by dropping baby after baby ... after baby at her door. Literally!

Lindsay is a featured author on Crosswalk.com and iBelieve.com, where she shares her life in devotional format. She can be found in Columbus, Ohio, where she spends most days with a messy puff of curls and a hot mug of Dandy Blend, chasing around her three wild kiddos, loving her hubby, and playing fetch with the tallest red labradoodle in Ohio.

Her hobbies include attempting to recreate her favorite restaurant recipes at home, creating gigantic charcuterie boards, starting 298 new books at the same time, fantasizing about owning her own apothecary, and cleaning up the same mess over and over again.

You can connect with Lindsay:

Website: LindsayTedder.com
Instagram: @lindsay.tedder
Facebook @lindsay.tedderspeaks

CHAPTER 12

Just Breathe

I WAS DEVASTATED. MY efforts to keep my tears at bay tested my patience as I attempted to refill my lungs. Devoid of windows, the tiny room was illuminated solely by harsh overhead fluorescents, casting an impersonal, transactional feel over its three inhabitants. When they spoke to me, their voices were kind and empathetic, in stark contrast with the room itself. Offers of assistance were uttered, kindnesses were offered, but I still couldn't fill my lungs in that clinical space.

Somehow, the conversation ended. I slowly made my way back to my desk, operating purely on muscle memory. As I approached my desk, I paused. I looked across my desk with tear-filled eyes at my boss sitting across from my seat. Back then, we secured our laptops when we were not at our desks to avoid the laptops growing legs and wandering off. As a result, each desk held a cable secured to the desk to anchor the laptop to its docking station. I locked my laptop to my desk with that cable, handed the key to my boss, and walked out of the doors I had wholeheartedly believed would guide my exit upon retiring in twenty-something years.

In my desperate need to completely fill my lungs for the first time since I received the mandate to come into the office, I gulped the open air. I couldn't get enough! It felt as though I had been holding my breath for days. As the humid summer air rushed into my lungs, my tenuous control over my tear ducts suffered a catastrophic failure. It was as if my first full breath gave me the air required to sob.

My livelihood was now a thing of the past. *Poof!* Gone. As a single mom, how would I support my family? Would we be homeless? Would I lose my kids? How would I make sure their bellies stayed full? My head began to spin as I wondered about the specifics of life as an unemployed single mom who entered her career later in life. I lacked the experience of others my age. Panic set in.

My breathing became fast and shallow, and my heart pounded out a frantic beat as I recounted those endless hours of writing code in my college classes, fighting to fully understand concepts. I relived the anxiety of the pressure I placed upon myself to ensure not only passing grades but grades that allowed me to graduate with honors despite being pregnant with my second child, a child who would require surgery at only two weeks old. I recalled the nights spent working well into dawn, ensuring all assignments were handed in prior to her surgery. My mind clamored with memories of endless dedication that allowed me to be free from control and support my children on my own. I had worked so hard—made so many sacrifices—just to end up *here*? Unemployed, alone, and terrified?! That couldn't be right. I couldn't reconcile my hard work, which seemed to be guided by God's own hand, with the uncertainty of what just happened. So, I spent the next few hours talking to God.

Well, "talking" is probably not the most accurate description. In reality, I was questioning God. Railing at Him. Asking Him, "Why?" in a variety of ways without bothering to stop and listen for an answer. Somehow, my petulant self became convinced God owed me an answer. My anger became a storm cloud, swirling over me, pregnant with moisture in the form of unshed tears and charged with lightning flashes of panic. Circling. It sealed my mind and my ears to God's voice.

But God is persistent.

In the following days, He revealed things to me. I found my identity in work, not Him. I placed so much emphasis on being a good employee that I had no time, energy, or desire for anything else—even God. My job, my gift from God, became too important.

Work had become my idol. Even worse, I'd thrown a temper tantrum with God because He didn't leave my idol intact. Wow. *Facepalm! Entitled much, Stef?*

Exodus 20:3 reminds us that we should have no other gods, yet I had made work a god, displacing capital-G God from His rightful throne. Of course, my lowercase-g god had to be removed. I recall signs—reminders—that I wasn't spending enough time with Jesus. Little inklings. Tiny nudges. He was trying to get my attention. Yet I repeatedly turned away from the reminders, choosing to ignore them so I could prove my worth to everyone watching.

Little did I realize I already had worth simply because I was alive. God created me on purpose for His purpose. A list of tasks was created for me before I was created (Ephesians 2:10). He chose me to complete these works. He didn't choose someone else to complete my assigned tasks. He chose *me*. I believed I wasn't worthy to do His work, so I tried to prove I was "good enough" by overachieving and seeking the approval of others. I forgot my identity wasn't my job title. My identity was given to me by God. Things I quickly remembered after spending time in His presence, time spent being still and listening for Him to teach me about Himself.

The fears began to subside as I spent more time in communion with Jesus than ever before. The lack of distraction was a welcome change and a timely gift. I began to believe He would make a way for me. We would get through this because I was walking with God. Suddenly, I was scheduled for an interview, and my panic returned. I had an overwhelming urge to take whatever job came my way to alleviate the financial concerns, so I went.

Had I not been desperate, I never would have accepted this interview. The role required no leadership skills, no independent thought, and no creativity. I viewed it as repetitive and mundane, a waste of my skill set. And yet, I accepted the interview and spent time anxiously wishing for an offer.

The offer certainly came, but not on that day. The pay was decent, they were impressed with what I would bring to the role, and the work was in an area where I excelled, but the thought of actually doing the job became too much to bear. My desperation warred with my faith. My urge to have a steady J-O-B was more appealing than waiting for a role that better employed my talents. When the panic cleared, I realized there was peace in declining the position. Naturally, I didn't trust the peace. I thought it was a ploy to lull me further into uncertainty. But it was an unshakable peace. When I thought of accepting the role, I was filled with anxiety, but when I entertained the option of declining, I felt peace. Weird.

I finally declined the offer. I trusted God despite what made sense to my brain. I remained an unemployed single mom with no choice but to trust God. And yet, the peace remained. I finally felt like a child of God rather than a single mom stressing about finding a position to support her children or finding my identity in my career.

After another interview, I accepted a challenging and satisfying role. I kept my head down, learned everything I could, and thought of ways to improve my skill set. I gave my best effort but didn't work every minute of the day anymore. I clocked out and went home at the end of the day. This was in stark contrast to the sixty and seventy-hour work weeks at the previous employer. I worked all those hours, putting my faith in my job to be viewed as a valuable, go-to resource, but I was let go and let down. I felt worthless and discarded, as though I added no value despite my hard work and commitment when the job ended, which was a devastating blow to my confidence. The new role was a refreshing change, as I was challenged and finally had a work-life balance.

After a year, I was offered a leadership role. I had done my job, and although I didn't feel as though I had done any leading, the team and hiring manager saw my skill set and potential. I hadn't even wanted to work for this employer strictly because of its location, but I finally agreed to be placed there on a temporary assignment. That role, my friend, opened the door to my dream job, a job not even offered at my previous employer. God answered my prayers.

I kept a healthy balance between work and home, spent time talking to God, and spent time listening to God too. I read His Word and, for the first time, could digest it. I even had time to lead Bible studies and serve others.

My dream job was certainly not easy, but I saw God in it every day. There were blessings, and there were challenges. There were days I had to "pray on my armor." You know, talk myself through Ephesians 6 and visualize myself personally donning each implement Paul mentioned to deflect those fiery arrows of hate being flung my way. But I was close enough to God to allow Him to fight the battles for me. He has never lost a fight!

When people went on the offensive against me, I prayed for them—genuine prayers. I asked God to give me His eyes to see people as He saw them. I asked Him to allow me to forgive others as He forgave me. I asked Him to show me how to love people as He loves them. I thanked Him for my job and all my other blessings. I thanked Him for the rejections as well as the rewards. I did my best to honor Him.

And things began to change.

People saw me in a positive light, but I wasn't performing any Clark Kent heroics to make them think more of me. I spent more time with Jesus and made every effort to become more like Him. Whether they realized it or not, I believe they saw Him through me because I was so intent on living life in tandem with the Lord.

I learned how to have an identity in Christ rather than in my work. I prioritized work, for sure, but it didn't take over my life. I understood the balance between who I was and what I did and realized they were not the same thing. I met others at work whose faith guided them, connected with them, and learned from them.

These days, things are noisier. Phones chime, socials notify, and tasks pile up. This world is definitely "worldin'." As I focus on the things Jesus is calling me to walk in, distractions abound. Through injuries and stressors, moves, and global crises, many shiny objects have been vying for my attention. But none of those shiny objects form my identity.

In truth, there are many days I fumble, stumble, and mumble, but I find those are usually the days I've missed my time with God. It's easier when I spend time in His Word, seeking His presence, and talking to Him throughout my day. It's easier to face the tough stuff. It's easier to remember He chose me as His daughter. There are still hard things to face, but it's easier to face them when I go to Him first.

I cannot serve both God and man. Idols must be laid at the foot of the cross. Jesus must be at the center of our lives, but idols unseat Him. I tend to overachieve. I recognize my tendency to try and earn my place. I try to remember throughout each day that my identity is found in Him. It's not a one-and-done kind of thing but a process where we sometimes have to remind ourselves of who He called us to be.

We tend to think of idols as secular items, but this is not the case. If we serve for the wrong reasons, service becomes an idol. If we place a checkmark next to reading our Bibles, then that task becomes an idol too. Only when Jesus sits on the throne of our hearts do we do things for the right reasons and keep idolatry in check.

Friend, finding time for "just one more thing" in this busy world is intimidating. But the days that start and end with Jesus are the most peaceful. When I was at my most vulnerable and unable to see how things could possibly work out, time with Jesus was the most valuable part of my full day. I often need to remind myself that despite my bursting-at-the-seams calendar, the moments seeking Him allow me to endure the craziness surrounding me.

Take a moment and think about a situation where you couldn't see a way out. Maybe it was parallel to my story, and you found yourself caught up by life's events as they swept you up in its raging currents. Perhaps it was a family issue. Was there a need to flee an abusive situation? Did you struggle over the loss of a loved one? Whatever your story holds, my friend, Jesus walks beside you. Can you find Him in your story as I found Him in mine?

None of those events formed your identity. They added to your story, yes, but they don't comprise your God-given identity. Wherever you find yourself today, remember that God calls you a masterpiece (Ephesians 2:10), a chosen people (1 Peter 2:9), a being created in His image (Genesis 1:27), and His child (John 1:12). These things help to form your identity, friend. You are not what you do, the mistakes you have made, who others say you are, or even what has happened to you.

You. Are. His.

About the Author

STEPHANIE WEBER IS AN Ohio native (O-H!) with a love for all things Buckeye. As a single mom of two adult children and three quirky rescue animals, Stef has recently rediscovered her creativity, which was buried under a lifetime of insecurities.

She is a survivor of various types of abuse and has lived with impostor syndrome for decades.

One of her greatest joys these days is playing the role of grandmother to her two precious granddaughters.

Stephanie is a roller coaster aficionado who loves a good rush of adrenaline. Her hobbies include reading, writing, painting, making a mess in the kitchen during her "creative process," and forgetting what she came into the room to do. From time to time, her ADHD adds a new hobby (or seven).

Stef is passionate about reminding women of their identity in Christ and has led women's Bible study groups for both adults and teens.

She loves to make others smile, and although she is a hard-core introvert, she plays the role of "class clown" effortlessly around those she knows well.

Stephanie is learning to love the person God created her to be, even when it's uncomfortable. She is committed to healing from her past and sharing her journey with others who wish to do the same.

Connect with Stephanie at:

Website: StephanieRWeber.com
Email: hello@stephanierweber.com
Instagram: @stephanie.r.weber
Facebook: @stephanie.r.weber1

CHAPTER 13

Turn Trials into a Triumphant Testimony

NOTHING HAD CHANGED. THE chair was still hard, the temperature was still freezing, and the lights were still blinding. Despite the machines making their usual humming noises, the silence was deafening. The familiar scent of antiseptic was almost comforting. Our ER visits always happened during the middle of the night, and the lack of activity in the hallways made me feel isolated.

For years, I felt like I was stranded on an island alone. Not the tropical kind with the giant palm trees and the perfect temperature we all dream about, where we're on the beach enjoying a gentle breeze without a care in the world. This was an island I wanted to escape from. There was no warmth on my skin, no relaxing waves of the ocean, and there never seemed to be a time when the weight of the circumstances was removed from my shoulders. It was far from paradise.

She slept as I watched, waiting for the rise and fall of her chest. I learned to detect the slightest change. COPD and blood clots became the opponent we battled endlessly.

I did not know this visit was the beginning of the end. The end of my years as a caretaker to the one who had given birth to me. My mom, the one who was supposed to have my back, love me unconditionally, and enjoy her life as I entered adulthood and began my own. My mom, the woman who inflicted years of emotional and mental pain through the last twenty-five years of our lives. The Lord called me to fill the role of her advocate in medical crises, her chauffeur to appointments, and her target when she was angry. And she was angry *a lot*.

As I sat there scared and alone, I repeated the Lord's promise to His children over and over again in my head. "I will never leave you nor forsake you" (Joshua 1:5, NIV). The peace that only the Lord can provide comforted me. I knew I was honoring Him as I navigated the unplanned journey of caring for my mom. He knew how complicated it was to let go of all my emotions as I surrendered my plans for His. Thankfully, I felt His presence.

I loved my mom. Our journey together was not always so unpleasant. We spent time together for many years, sharing laughter and good times. Mondays were my off days, and we spent a lot of them together, going to the mall and doing activities with my small children. Some days, we sat at her kitchen table with an ice-cold glass of sweet tea. Those were the good times. But then, several tragic things happened in a very short time.

- She grieved the loss of her mother.

- She grieved the loss of her special needs son.

- She grieved the end of her thirty-two-year marriage.

When the storms of life overcame her, I became her emotional support system. It wasn't easy to be her only source of support and confidante. I was not equipped to support her emotionally through all her losses.

During these life-changing events, I came to know the Lord. A friend shared that Jesus loves me and wants to be my Lord and Savior. A simple prayer to the Lord acknowledging that I wanted to surrender my heart and life to Him began a new life with Him. I want to share that with you today.

As a result of my decision, Jesus was the One who brought me comfort. He taught me forgiveness, how to trust and love Him, and how to leave the negative thoughts behind despite the hard times. Matthew 11:28–30 (NIV) tells us, "Come to me, all who are weary and burdened, and I will give you rest. Take my yoke upon you and learn from me, for I am gentle and humble in heart, and you will find rest for your souls. For my yoke is easy and my burden is light." Our hearts change when we surrender our lives to Him, even when the circumstances do not.

One day, as I shared Jesus with my mom, she told me she had come to know the Lord at a young age. However, even with the Lord, she could not reach a place of forgiveness and resolve bitterness. With my new relationship with Christ, I was able to forgive and restore my relationship with my dad, find joy in life, and enjoy the peace that surpasses all understanding.

The camaraderie of anger between us regarding the ending of her marriage with my dad seemed to bring her validation for the bitterness she maintained. Unknowingly, I became an enabler, helping her refuse to move on with her life. Our journey together through life was forever changed when she could not accept that I did not have the same mindset as her anymore. She resented my new "rose-colored glasses" that faith had produced, and my ability to forgive placed a wedge in our relationship.

She became lost and alone in her own private island of grief, pain, despair, and bitterness.

Instead of seeking comfort and claiming the promises of the Lord, she continued on her path of anger. She chose retaliation, and I became her target.

Through the years, she was manipulative in our relationship. I didn't recognize it at first. Surely, my own mom wouldn't do these things intentionally to bring anguish upon me. She demanded my time, my attention, and my devotion. She disconnected herself from others, making me her sole support. I believe it was a test to see if I would abandon her, although I proved I wasn't going anywhere.

She tested me, and I always passed. She felt the world abandoned her and wanted to see if I would also.

She needed to feel loved, and standing by her proved I loved her. She knew my strength was from the Lord. She tried to bait me to see if she could provoke my old self to reappear. Only through God's grace and mercy could I resist the thoughts and words of my past bitterness and anger. I counted to ten a lot. She accused me of giving her the silent treatment, and I shared that my silence was to avoid saying anything I would regret.

In Ephesians 6:11–13, the Bible tells us to put on the whole armor of God so we can stand and resist the enemy. I am convinced the division of the relationship between me and my mother was exactly what was behind this battle. My mom couldn't fight for us. She was too broken to defend us. So, it was my challenge to face. I relied on God's belt of truth, His breastplate of righteousness, His shoes of peace, His shield of faith, the helmet of salvation, and His Word, the sword of the Spirit. At times, it was a simple prayer: "Lord, please deafen my ears and anoint my tongue."

Those were tough years, but the Lord brought me through. In hindsight, I realize the Lord was equipping me to rely on the fruit of the Spirit in Galatians 5:22—love, joy, peace, patience, kindness, goodness, faithfulness, gentleness, and self-control.

- I showed up for her out of **love** and the **joy** of the Lord.

- I endured the anger and bitterness with **peace** and **patience**.

- As I sacrificed time with my husband, children, and grandchildren, the Lord gave me **kindness** and **goodness**.

- When days didn't go as planned, God filled me with **faithfulness** and **gentleness**.

- When the urge to retaliate came upon me, the Lord gave me **self-control**.

I am thankful for the opportunities the Lord gave me to learn and grow in the attributes of the Holy Spirit.

It's been over ten years since she's been gone; I still hear her in my ears sometimes. I still grieve for the life she chose not to live. It comforts me to believe the Lord welcomed His hurting child home. She now has the peace she could not enjoy here on earth.

The Lord continued to teach me as He called me to honor my mom and write her eulogy. It was a gift to be able to share with the ones who did not know her before she succumbed to sadness and grief. I shared about her strength when she rode a bus to the state capitol to fight for help for special needs children. I shared the times she was our Girl Scout leader, teaching us how to cook hot dogs on a stick over a fire and roast marshmallows. There were many stories to share of her years of better times. It was important to me for her legacy to reflect the good memories of her life.

The ER visits are a thing of the past; the lessons linger, reminding me of the difficult journey. The harsh lights and cold rooms are gone, replaced by the light of the Lord and the warmth of His love. I have the gift of peace that comes from knowing I did my best.

Even now, as new trials come and the days are tough, I am reminded of His promise in Joshua 1:5 (NIV): "I will never leave you nor forsake you." Again, the Lord reaches down from heaven, holds my hand, and carries me through.

I am thankful for those days when He shaped me into a stronger person, ready to face whatever comes next. Those memories remind me that things in life may take me by surprise, but life never surprises Him.

As we allow Him to work in our hearts and lives, He will transform our trials into a beautiful testimony to encourage others. James 1:12 (ESV) says, "Blessed is the man who remains steadfast under trial, for when he has stood the test He will receive the crown of life, which God has promised to those who love him."

This is a poem the Lord laid on my heart for my mom.

I had a little chat with Jesus; I told Him about you:
"It is so hard to see my mama sad and blue.
Life has been a bumpy road with dark and cloudy skies,
I wish I did not see the sadness when I look into her eyes.
Now I stand before you, Lord, to intercede for her.
I know that if I ask for it, a miracle will occur.
Please fill her with the peace and joy that only You can give,
the sweet life that You offer, I want to see her live."
Then the Lord He spoke to me; He whispered in my ear:
"I have so much to say to her, things she needs to hear.
I can take away her anguish and take away her pain.
I am here beside her, have her call upon My name.
There is not a single moment, a minute, or a day
that I have not been there with her and seen her on her way.
Please tell her that I know her sacrifice and loss,
I, too, have lost a son; I paid a heavy cost.
Each and every trial I allowed her to go through
is meant to give her courage when someone else will wear her shoes.
There is a job I have for her—a mission to fulfill;
it will bring her many blessings if she only will.
I want her to reach out and serve others in My name,
the sad, the weary, hopeless, the broken, and the lame.
As she reaches out and finds others to lift up,
she will know My peace and joy as I fill her cup."

About the Author

CINDY MORTON EGGER HAS spent most of her life using her God-given ability as an artist to share her faith. Her work has been sold in gift shops around the country and featured in several national magazines. Her entrepreneurial spirit led to the creation of her business "Steps of Faith Inspirational Gifts." She sells a full line of gifts in person at artisan markets and online. This gives her the opportunity to share her testimony and love for the Lord with thousands of people. She loves to share heartwarming and humorous stories but realizes there are times when the hard stories need to be told. She embraces the opportunity to listen and comfort the hurting people the Lord puts in her path.

She published an interactive devotional journal, *Finding the Lord Every Day in Unexpected Ways*, which launched as a top new release in three categories on Amazon. Cindy's love to minister, inspire, and encourage others shines throughout her work. The devotional features her art and reflects the hearts and concerns of many people she ministered to during her forty years as a hairstylist. You will enjoy how this devotional creates a fresh new way to find Jesus every day.

With no plans to slow down, Cindy is creating more written projects and enjoys speaking and storytelling opportunities about her life in the South. She shares about her transformed life when she learned that "good isn't good enough" to spend eternity with the Lord and how simple words and actions can be powerful and life-changing. You will hear transparency, honesty, and humor in a relatable way that will make you feel like a trusted friend.

She loves to embrace life and learn new things. Although she doesn't know yet how the Lord will incorporate her latest hobby, learning to play the drums, into her ministry, she is convinced He will. Bobby, her husband and first and only groupie, is her biggest supporter. He never knows what adventure she will take him on next. Their kids just shake their heads at her antics and ideas, and the grandchildren think she is cool.

Visit her website to see all she has to offer.

Register for her newsletter to stay current with all her adventures at CindyMortonEgger.com and stepsoffaith.com

Instagram: @stepsoffaithbycindy
Facebook: Steps of Faith Inspirational Gifts

Her book, *Finding the Lord Every Day in Unexpected Ways*, is available on Amazon at: https://amzn.to/4cQ4wKN.

CHAPTER 14

Not the Same, but Good

WEARY OF MY HOUSE search and hope waning, I stepped into the foyer of the next real estate listing.

Cue the sparkly fog and angelic music. I breathed deeply and immediately knew I was home.

It was everything I wanted. The open floor plan and generous placement of windows provided a cheerful frame for the backyard that mimicked a tropical resort. Four soaring palm trees anchored the corners of the pool. A lush assortment of flowering shrubs connected a beautiful fig tree in one corner and a lemon tree ladened with giant-sized fruit in the other.

It was perfection. In summer, squeals of laughter bounced off the pool. Quiet conversations floated around the firepit's soft glow in the cool breezes of autumn evenings. Winters were gentle and short. Life was good!

Then came the Great Texas Freeze of 2021.

My not-so-Southern friends might laugh at our thin-skinned lack of tolerance to the bitter cold. But the combination of winds and frigid temperatures overloaded our infrastructure, causing power outages, water supply issues, economic disruption, and extreme hardship for our residents.

My tropical paradise succumbed to the prolonged arctic blast, leaving my yard looking like a desolate and deserted wasteland. I hung to the short-lived hope as my treasured palm trees began to show brief signs of life. My heart still grieves the day those towering queens were cut from their thrones, leaving an imposing vacancy in my yard. The flowering shrubs that once danced softly in the summer's breeze left no trace of their former glory, leaving my heart longing for the lush clusters of flora and fauna.

Planting again. Freezing again.

I watched as seasons came and went. Despair set in, and I couldn't bring myself to plant again in what seemed an act of futility. How could I ever recreate the beauty that once graced my backyard? What use was there to even try?

Just plants, you say. But what about when it's not?

Years of disappointing relationships littered the landscape of my past. Weary of the search and hope waning, I was introduced to a man. Dare I hope this was "the one?"

Cue the sparkly fog and angelic music.

He was everything I wanted. Tall, dark, and handsome. Loved Jesus. Wickedly funny and could turn mundane situations into a brilliantly told story. His eyes danced when he looked at me. Thoughtful gestures assured me I was on his mind throughout the day. Conversation flowed effortlessly, extracting deeply embedded secrets of our souls and healing us both in ways we didn't know we needed. He inspired me to fall in love with the music I had discarded years before as we spent hours singing and playing together, he on his guitar and me on the keyboard.

Life was wonderful.

My world was beautiful and well-ordered.

- Great new job.

- Devoted daughter and beloved son-in-love expecting my third perfect grandson.

- Beautiful home just down the sidewalk from them.

- Handsome sweetheart who adored me.

And then came the knock on my door.

The perfection of my life evaporated in an instant. My heart raced as two police officers stood on my front porch. I made a mental inventory of the whereabouts of those I loved and tried to think of anything I might have done that warranted a visit from the police at this hour. Perhaps there was suspicious behavior in the neighborhood. They must be doing a courtesy check of the area.

My fears were refueled when they asked if my name was Pam Mitchael.

"Yes." I nodded.

"Do you know Donnie D?"

"Yes." Fear began to boil into my throat.

I listened to his next words through a fog of disbelief as they tumbled out like bombs exploding in my heart.

"Found unresponsive."

"You'll need to call this number and speak with the coroner."

"Is there someone who can come and be with you?"

Make them stop! I stumbled back from the police officer delivering this soul-crushing message.

"What is your relationship to him?"

How could I describe all he was to me in this fear-filled moment? My sweetheart, my confidant. My best friend, the love of my life. The one who helped restore my battered heart and brought music back into my life. The one who renewed my hope for "happily ever after." That's what I *wanted* to say.

"He's my boyfriend," is all I could manage through the choking grip of grief.

My head was spinning, my stomach churning. I didn't know whether to sit or stand or walk when everything in me wanted to run. Run away from the horror story unfolding into my devastating reality. Close the door and refuse to open it again to the delivery of such pain.

As the endless night wore on, I retreated, again and again, to my "war room," a closet I had designated for the purpose of prayer several months before. There, I cried out to God, not with questions of "why" but with a plea that He would somehow receive glory in and through it. I journaled this prayer in three separate entries: "Don't let this be wasted."

The next day, as my pastor prayed over me, he stopped in the middle of his prayer and spoke words I will cherish for the entirety of my life.

"I don't know if this makes any sense to you, but God keeps showing me this over and over, like flashing neon signs—*not wasted*."

Those were my words! The words I prayed *to Him*, now delivered back to me straight from the heart of my Father through my pastor. Those words are an anchor for my faith that His gaze is forever on me. They stabilize my emotions in the moments when I feel like waves of grief might overtake me. They remind me these momentary trials are so brief in the light of eternity.

He can bring purpose from our pain. It is not wasted.

I don't know what the future holds, but I certainly know Who holds it. In the meantime, I am clothed in strength and dignity, and I can laugh without fear of the future (Proverbs 31:25).

What losses have you suffered? Whether it's something as trivial as a lost plant or as soul-crushing as the death of a loved one, Jesus cares. Rest assured, it is not wasted. He sees your broken heart, and only He can mend it. Psalm 34:18 (NIV) declares, "The Lord is close to the brokenhearted and saves those who are crushed in spirit." Lean into Him and allow Him to comfort you. Things may never be the same as they were before or even the way we dreamed they might be. But we can hold fast to the promise of Isaiah 43:19 (NLT). "For I am about to do something new. See, I have already begun! Do you not see it? I will make a pathway through the wilderness. I will create rivers in the dry wasteland."

Oh ... and my yard? I am looking out over a newly planted row of flowering shrubs, colorful flower beds, a gazebo in one corner, and a pergola with a fire pit and hammocks summoning me to relax and enjoy the new view.

It's not the same, but it sure is good.

About the Author

SPEAKER. WRITER. TRUTH SEEKER. **Pam Mitchael** loves Jesus. She is the Director of the Christian Communicators Conference, a training conference for speakers. Her passion is encouraging women to realize their true value and identity in Christ.

She's still on the fence about whether she is a city girl born in the country or a country girl living in the city, but has never forgotten where she came from.

She can often be found baking cookies with her three grandsons, thrift shopping, and road-tripping with friends. Pink peonies, finding a great bargain, and sneaking a bowl of Blue Bell Pistachio Almond ice cream are among her favorite things as she follows Jesus on this journey called life.

You can connect with Pam by email at: pam@pammitchael.com
Website: pammitchael.com
Facebook: @pmitchael

CHAPTER 15

Grace in the Heartache

A Pastor's Wife's Rejection and Restoration

I was so excited to leave my job and start my dream career in photography—a dream that was crushed within a week. My husband is a pastor and some of the church leaders approached him and said, "We want you to resign immediately." They wanted the church to go in a different direction and decided we were in the way. We were not allowed to say goodbye at the next service or explain why we would no longer be there.

They asked us to pack up Ellis' office and leave. Blindsided and betrayed by people we trusted and ministered alongside for over a decade, we packed up my husband's office and walked out. We'd served in ministry for thirty-five years, and this was the first time a small group decided our day of departure before we did, leaving us jobless and speechless.

We knew almost everyone in our small town but felt alone and rejected—unjustified outcasts. Although I took it personally, the attack was directed at my husband, not me. To add to the anguish, our young adult children became disillusioned with the church as they experienced the hurt right alongside us. We attempted to shield them from rumors that could cause them more despair, but we could not shield their hearts.

They knew their dad had never spoken unkindly about anyone and was always available for the church families' personal and emotional needs, even at the expense of missing our own family activities. They understood their dad's calling and life as a pastor and were always supportive. They witnessed him loving the church family and only preaching from the Word. And yet, they saw him being treated poorly. Through it all, our family stood together, united in our love and support for one another.

The question of "why" turned to "how" could they do that to us? How could they think that upon their decision, it was time for us to leave? Where was God consulted in this? Where were the prayers of godly people to rally around and see how God wanted this to be handled? I always knew God was not the author of confusion, yet we were right in the middle of one of the most significant life changes, full of hurt, disappointment, and chaos.

God held our hands, yet my faith was weak instead of strong. He knew what was happening, and I needed to wait on Him, but I continued to wonder what was next. Thoughts about how we would financially make ends meet stole my peace. I wondered if God would place us with another church family to serve, and the wondering went on and on. I wish I could say I placed my faith more in Him, but instead, I worried. I became self focused instead of Jesus focused.

One day, as I lay on the floor, stretched out, pleading with God to make this all disappear, He spoke to my heart. He showed me He was still near and that my faithfulness would be rewarded in due time. So, I waited. It may not have been what I wanted to hear, but it was what I needed.

As we navigated the hurt and confusion, I watched my husband, Ellis, with admiration. Despite the pain, he remained firm, his faith unwavering. It seemed he healed from this experience relatively quickly, although I could sense his concern for me and my struggle to let go of my bitterness. I believe he withheld some of his pain because of my insecurities. I had left my job to pursue my dream as a photographer, but it became necessary for me to return to work to supplement our income, which added more bitterness to what I was already feeling. He didn't want to heap his turmoil on me.

I knew deep down that God could change things if He wanted to. He could change all this with one swift hand, but it was not His plan for now. My heart was still bitter as months passed, and I expressed little forgiveness.

During this challenging period, I was blessed to have a circle of close friends in town who provided unwavering support. They checked on me, took me to lunch, and prayed for me. They sent me Scriptures to encourage and uplift me, reminding me that I was not alone in my struggle. But even with the support of my friends, I continued to cling to my hurt and bitterness, using them as a shield against any further pain. I may have looked like I had it together, but deep in my heart, the pain was so raw and hurtful, and I was struggling.

As I worked through this spiritual warfare, I realized I was not where I needed to be in my relationship with the Lord. I could see that my walk with the Lord was lacking commitment. I struggled with this because had I walked closer with God, I would have realized that this was a battle for Him alone. It was a turning point in both my husband's and my life to rely on Him and practice what we preached, and I was failing miserably.

As I began to pray about asking God to change me, forgive my thoughts, and help me believe that He was enough, I knew I needed to forgive the ones who hurt us. However, I couldn't do it alone. I needed God's help. I needed to trust in His plan. And I needed to trust He would provide for our family. I was lost in Satan's grip, and it was time to stop.

After several weeks of not being in God's house with His people, we decided we needed to be in church somewhere. I was very reluctant to go, but I knew what I was doing was not working or pleasing to God. I knew that part of healing was to be where we could be healed. We returned to a friend's church near our town and were involved as much as possible for about a year, allowing God to heal the open wounds. Serving others is another way we got back on track. Being with other fellow believers sets us up for success. Putting our worries, hurts, and future in God's hands brings great comfort.

God reminded me that He wanted more of me. I felt Him drawing me closer, calling me to trust Him more deeply. After wrestling with this for a couple of weeks, searching Scripture, and waiting in His presence, I thought of my friend of twenty-five years, Karla Byrd. I shared my despair with her and sought her advice. After a long conversation, she handed me a book by Lysa TerKeurst entitled *What Happens to Women When They Say Yes to God*. As I read this book, I noticed it aligned with Scripture, and God was leading me in a new direction by softening my heart and showing me how to follow Him more intentionally than ever. I felt like one of the disciples, trusting Jesus when He said, "Follow me."

I realized other pastors' wives likely felt like I did—alone, rejected, and without support. They probably feel like they are in the fishbowl, hesitant to be who they are, becoming withdrawn, and losing focus without anyone to talk to. Although I have known for years I wanted to connect with other pastors' wives and help them heal, I wasn't sure it was God's plan. Previously, I used many excuses not to follow what my heart longed for, but I became convinced and at peace it was the right time.

My calling to encourage women is abundantly life-giving. It is so satisfying to see God work in the lives of other women, share what I have learned, and assure them there is more positive in life than negative. There is joy in the Lord. Nehemiah 8:10 tells us that joy in the Lord is our strength. When we place our faith and trust in Him, He strengthens us to weather life's storms.

Sometimes, it takes a while to see what God is doing when our lives fall apart, seemingly dismantled by others, but rest assured, He puts it all back together. As Jesus' followers, we are not exempt from hurt and disappointment. But how we handle it is our choice. As we read the Bible, we learn how Jesus handled betrayal, and we can pray for the strength to imitate Him—serve as He served and forgive as He forgave.

God knows you; He created you and is fighting battles for you. He has not forgotten you. Forgive and let your hard hurt turn into a healed heart. Don't miss what God has in store for you, how you can grow, and how you can watch Him fight the battle to forgive those who have hurt you.

> Trust in the Lord with all your heart, and lean not on your understanding; In all your ways acknowledge Him, and He shall direct your paths.
>
> Proverbs 3:5–6 (NKJV)

About the Author

JACKIE HAYDEN HAS WALKED through battles and come out on fire for the Lord. She is a women's speaker, author, and Bible teacher. She loves to share encouraging messages with other minister's wives and women from all walks of life.

In her spare time, you can find her looking through the lens of a camera, capturing special moments, living life with her husband, Ellis, who is a pastor, and enjoying her family and friends. Her Yorkie, Willow, is the princess of the home, and Jackie loves her fiercely.

Jackie is a Texas woman teaching women all about Jesus.

Jackie can be reached through her website at Jackiehaydenspeaks.com
Email: jackiehayden4316@gmail.com

CHAPTER 16

The Joy of His Presence

A MOTHER'S JOURNEY TO FIND A FUTURE AFTER LOSS

I HAD BEEN HERE before, surrounded by boxes waiting to be unpacked. I met the challenge before me with both excitement and wonder. Excitement, knowing we were finally in our new home; wonder, knowing I would once again find items filled with precious memories, reminding me of blessings in my life, places I had been, and people left behind as a military spouse. And so, the day began. Box one, done. Box two, empty. And then—the phone call no parent wants to receive.

Eleven hundred miles away, our son was in a one-car accident and was being Life Flighted to a major hospital. Time stood still. A mental image of David at two years old filled my mind, precocious and full of life. Yet, in those moments, somehow, my heart knew his earthly life would soon be over. I stood in front of the linen closet where I was unpacking and looked at the next item. It was a potholder with our three sons' handprints on it. Lifting it to my face, I touched the tiny handprint of David, kissed it, and prayed.

What else can a mother do when a child's life is drifting between this earth and eternity? It was the strangest prayer. "Lord, You know what's best. You know I want David to be healed and with us for many more years. Yet, if he will be tormented by what the outcome of his accident will mean physically or mentally—well, God, You know him best. Please God ..." Amid the prayer, tears drenched the potholder clenched tightly in my hand.

There are no words to fill the void of those long moments waiting for the next update. Yet, it was as if I could see into the helicopter as they worked on our son. Three times, he was shocked as his heart stopped beating. I saw a battle for his life both physically and spiritually. I could see Jesus with him battling away the enemy. Then, the vision stopped, and I was again looking down at the potholder. The next call we received delivered the devastating news. David did not survive.

Gently laying the potholder on the shelf of the closet, with a house full of unpacked boxes, we prepared to leave for the long journey before us. On the road, my vision sometimes blurred from tears; I began to pray about what took place in the helicopter. "Lord, I need a sign David is with you. *Please*, God, my mama's heart needs to know David is with you." I cannot remember when it happened, but a rainbow appeared. It wasn't just any rainbow. This rainbow was bright and stayed first in front of me and then seemingly drifted off to the driver's side as it faded away.

It wasn't raining except for the tears that continued to fall. The day was clear, with a few cotton-like clouds decorating the deep blue sky. Yet, there it was—God's assurance to me. My heart began to feel an overwhelming sense of calm, and the Holy Spirit spoke silently to me, "For God so loved the world that He gave His only Son, that whoever believes in him should not perish but have eternal life" (John 3:16, RSV).

The rainbow and the verse collided within me. I knew. God was with David in the helicopter; He was with him and died for him. Can a mother find peace amid the death of her son? Only God can give the peace that passes understanding. That is what God gave to me on that long, unwanted journey.

Our son was not our only tragic loss. Prior to David's graduation to eternity, my brother was murdered, and my brother-in-law chose to end his life. I also experienced a traumatic brain injury from falling—an injury that necessitated my retirement from a large church where I ministered.

My future? I knew it was in God's hands. I prayed. I prayed again and again. "What now, Lord? My ability to process and retain information has been short-circuited. What do You want me to do? I feel useless for You."

I longed to hear from God. I waited, and I waited. My desire to hear from Him swelled, consuming my heart and soul. During those days and long weeks and months, God took me on a journey through Scripture, revealing stories of life and loss. One of the most poignant, sad, and God-redeemed stories that spoke to my heart during those dark days was the story of Ruth and Naomi. While each of us experiences different losses and responds to them differently, the combination of Ruth's and Naomi's journey through joy, loss, darkness, and redemption reminded me God sees_a way. God knows the way. He makes a way even if we cannot fathom a future.

Found in the book of Ruth in the Old Testament, Naomi's and Ruth's journey is a story for anyone who has lost a loved one or has had to move and leave family and friends behind. It is also the story of those who, like me, wonder, "What now?"

Happily married with two sons but experiencing a famine where they lived, Naomi and her husband, Elimelek, decided to travel from Bethlehem to Moab, a foreign country where there was food.

In the scope of ten years while they were in Moab, Naomi, an Israelite, lost her homeland, her husband, and both sons. Her life had been full but was now empty. Her losses were great, and because of those she lost, her sorrow resulted in feeling God brought the misfortunes upon her. She even rejected her name, Naomi, which means pleasant or gentle, and told people to call her Mara, which means bitter. Her losses created an embittered soul within her. She was miserable.

Ruth, the daughter-in-law not of Jewish culture or descent, lost her husband and was childless. When Naomi decided to leave Moab, Ruth chose to accompany Naomi to Bethlehem, leaving behind possible relatives, friends, and her homeland. We don't know much about Ruth at this point, but we do know her darkness was somehow tethered to hope in her choice to stay with Naomi rather than in the land where she grew up and might have easily remarried. Still, her trip with Naomi was one of leaving darkness into a future totally unknown. Perhaps she was desperate to leave the past behind. Perhaps she had experienced the God of Israel in the years of her marriage. Perhaps, unknowingly, she was being led by God away from darkness.

My own darkness came not only from the losses of my loved ones and the dreams and hopes I had, especially for my son, but also thinking I would forever be lost in a world without my short-term memory, a result of the fall. How would I be able to serve God? I had done all the therapy I could. I took medications to help my memory. While some healing took place, after two years I reached maximum healing and still had much memory loss.

Much like Naomi crying out to God in her grief and pain, I cried out to God to show me the way. Like her, I couldn't change the losses that changed my life. I couldn't go back and undo the decisions leading to the fall I experienced. There is much in life we cannot undo. My tears of pain, feeling useless, of having my life forever changed, went to God—over and over.

I have learned to say, "But God." In those dark times, God was with me, like He was with Naomi and Ruth. Each found new life and hope in ways they could have never dreamed. Because even in her grief, Naomi listened to her heart, and I believe the leading of God. Out of devastating circumstances came redemption. Eventually, Ruth married Boaz, a relative of Naomi's late husband. They had a son, Obed, who had a son, Jesse, who had a son, David, who became king of Israel, from whose lineage comes the King of Kings—Jesus.

Ruth reminds us that God transforms our lives, brings good out of difficulties, and gives us a beautiful example of how He takes a situation we believe is hopeless and turns it into something glorious. If you have lost a loved one and perhaps feel your future is hopeless, listen to what God can do. Even when we don't see a way, God will provide.

Looking back, while God gave me time to read Scripture and physically heal, He was at work.

It didn't happen immediately, but then, out of a deep sleep, God woke me up in the darkness of the night, and I knew I was to write. The urge to immediately get up was so powerful I could not ignore it. I went straight to my computer, where the words flowed like a rapid stream of clear water. They were words that sparkled with joy amid difficult times, words that told how God had worked light into darkness, and words of how God's presence had wrapped me like a warm blanket on a cold night.

Writing the first book was cathartic. As the words flew from my mind to the keyboard, tears stained my face. The words that flowed taught me so much about God, grief, loss—and His unconditional love, His ability to bring good out of difficult and tragic situations, and most of all, His faithfulness.

As the book, *Grief: The Unwanted Journey*, was being edited and prepared for publication, God began to show me how many people around me were grieving. I started to share about my journey of healing, which, as those who have experienced great loss know, never ends but does get better and better until it settles as a part of our God story. God continued to open my heart to tell how my story was God's story, just like Naomi's and Ruth's story became God's story of redemption from darkness to light. I finally saw how God wanted me to surrender my future focus to Him and allow Him to direct what my future would be for Him. I was set on a course to share my story.

But God. God's plans are so much bigger than ours! Just when I was getting comfortable with what I thought my future held, God put another book on my heart. *Really God?* I wasn't sure I wanted to relive the pain of those first few years of grief. Grief has a way of making the holidays difficult. When I started this book, I realized it wasn't supposed to be about how to get through the holidays but how to survive them with a new focus. It was to share God's desire for us to find joy amid grief through His transformational love. The words were to acknowledge deep grief while finding ways to celebrate precious memories.

Once again, I wrote. And while writing, I saw God was not through with *my* healing journey yet. That's how good God is! God didn't want me, nor does He want anyone, to have places of pain He has not touched with His healing. I am so glad God showed me new ways to bring celebration into memories and continue to include the love I shared with those I have lost in every holiday.

Several years have passed since God downloaded those words, those stories, into my heart and onto the pages of my first book. Little did I know God had more books in mind. I knew He was not finished, because since writing *Surviving the Holidays While Grieving*, God put a desire in my heart to write a book for children who struggle with grief over loss. God divinely appointed coauthor Michelle Medlock Adams to provide the words children would understand, while I wrote a layer for adults to help the children process their loss.

Are there more books to come? I don't know. But God. God knows. My journey is in His hands—the very hands that walked with me through the darkest days of my life and gave me the courage to face each day with new joy and expectation because, after all, He is always faithful to provide more than we could ever imagine.

While our lives can be turned upside down in a moment, God's desire for us, His great love for us, always guides us toward healing and futures filled with hope. Ultimately, when we give our grief and our struggles to God, He will guide us to once again find His perfect peace and inner joy.

About the Author

JANET K. JOHNSON IS an author, speaker, workshop leader, pastor, and spiritual formation mentor who considers herself to be most blessed to live in and spread the love of God. Having experienced many significant losses and tragedies, her passion is helping others draw close to God, especially during life's most difficult times. She rejoices when God catches her by surprise amid ordinary moments and knows it is God's joy within her that has enabled the difficult times to be filled with hope.

Janet holds BA, MSW, and MDiv degrees as well as certifications in spiritual formation and healing ministries. She participates in Aldersgate Renewal Ministries, the Walk to Emmaus, and the Order of St. Luke.

Janet and her husband of over fifty years live in North Carolina with their cavadoodle, Gracie. They have four grown children, one of whose life on earth was far too short. Janet cherishes time with her children and grandchildren.

Connect with Janet via email: joyfilledjan1@gmail.com
Website: janetkjohnson.com

CHAPTER 17

Starting Over

I SAT IN THE tiny room off to the side of the church, waiting for someone to tell me it was time to walk down the aisle. They say your wedding day is the most glorious day of your life, but I felt sick to my stomach. Was this wedding jitters? Was I overreacting? I would never know because no one was there with me to answer those questions or settle my nerves. I had no idea where my mom was at that point in my life. She came in and out of town and only looked me up when it suited her. She had been homeless for the last few years and was more interested in her next adventure than in how her children were handling life.

I grew up with a narcissistic mother who threw herself at men like a prize to be won. She won them, but they were not worth it. Most were abusive, and the ones who were actually nice, she dumped because she didn't know how gentleness felt. When she wasn't in abusive relationships, she turned the aggressiveness on us children. It was chaos all the time. These were the relationship lessons I learned and reflected on as I anxiously waited in that small room.

I sat in the room and tried to understand why I was feeling panicky. My guy was nice, not abusive. He loved me. We moved in together a few months before because I didn't know if I wanted to marry him—yet. I thought pretending we were a devoted couple would help me decide. He was a pretty good provider, and I knew for a fact he wanted children. We suffered a miscarriage a few months prior, and it was then that he proposed. That's love, right? So why were there alarm bells going off in my body when it should have been filled with blissful feelings of peace, joy, and happiness?

There were no answers that day. I didn't know God then, not in the way I heard most Christians talk about Him. I wondered, "Did God love a horrible person like me?" After all, I was a party girl who had done the same things I grew up learning: lead with your body, and hopefully, love will follow.

I hesitantly walked down the aisle with the biggest fake smile so I wouldn't hurt anyone's feelings. I shoved my emotions down because that's what you do when you are a young woman who has lived through childhood trauma. I learned that shutting down kept me safe for the moment. I knew in my heart this marriage was doomed from the start. Something felt off. What did I know?

I wasn't religious, but I threw up a prayer to a God who scared me, yet I still had a mustard seed of faith to ask for protection. Could He hear me? Did He care? Was I crazy for asking? Too late to wonder now ... I was married.

The next few months were wrought with one disaster after another. Nothing went right in this marriage. The biggest thing was the miscommunication, or, I should say, the lack of emotional care. He tried but was more concerned with his family's opinions than mine. His mother decided to move in with us just two months later. His sister, aunt, and cousin all lived on the same street as us. We never had a moment for ourselves. His comment was always, "They are just trying to help." He didn't want to face things alone with me; he wanted confirmation from them, and they always sided with him. Things came to a head six months into the marriage, and I walked out. So many things accumulated in the demise of this marriage, and my capacity to hold on left me. Then the unthinkable happened. I found out I was pregnant. I went back. It didn't get better, but I had a little being inside of me to love.

Our son was born on a cold night in January. He was perfect. But I found out three days later that his body was not. He was born with congenital heart disease and needed open heart surgery. I was too young for such big adult things. At twenty-six years old, I was thrown into a whirlwind of doctors, NICU, nurses, and too many decisions that once again made me feel I was being punished by a God who was mad at me and how I lived my life.

When you reach the end of yourself, you have two choices: You can keep making bad decisions forever because you give up, or you can cry out to a God you aren't even sure is listening. I did the second thing. I asked for a priest at the hospital. That day, I started a quest that I believed God was taking me on to draw me closer to Him.

My son passed away two weeks after he was born, and my marriage ended shortly thereafter. There was too much damage already done. It was too painful to be around my former husband. The statistics say 80 percent of marriages fall apart after the death of a child. Our odds were already stacked against us.

I believe sometimes you must lose it all to start something new. I didn't like it, but I knew I needed to figure out who I was without being tied to someone else. For the first time in my life, I was alone without a man. I also had no job or a place to live. What was this going to look like for me? Once again, silent prayers went up to the heavens. I needed help.

Can we trust God when there is nothing trustworthy in our lives? I asked out of fear, not because I trusted Him. Something in me was pulling me toward this force that felt different.

I called a friend and discovered her work was hiring, and she offered up her couch for a few months until I could get on my feet. Slow baby steps toward freedom and figuring out what I wanted my future to look like. After three months, I found my first apartment, and it felt like a little slice of heaven.

I wish I could say it was smooth sailing from there, but many more nights were spent crying on the floor, asking God what I was supposed to do. I never took adequate time to grieve for my son because I was too busy trying to trudge forward. I shoved my emotions down once again, trying to survive on my own. Parts of this journey felt calming, even though it was tumultuous at the same time. I needed the tears, the alone time, and the opportunity to make decisions on my own.

I felt I had messed up so badly in the marriage and baby department that God had certainly shut the door. I was okay with that. After a failed marriage, the craving to be a bride gets tarnished, and you don't want it anymore. I was settling into being comfortable with just me. A year went by. Then Mike showed up. This guy was sweet, gentle, caring, and took his time to make me feel confident and safe.

Six years after my first marriage ended, God slowly showed me grace and love with the right partner. Mike and I married. God drew me close when we had our first daughter, Ariel. She was perfect. I still suffered from trauma with this pregnancy, worrying that something would go wrong. When I became pregnant with our second daughter, Dominique, I felt God pulling me toward Him even more. I started talking to my daycare provider, which led me to a church, and for the first time, I felt His complete love. I became a Christian that day and never looked back. I asked God to protect this baby inside of me, as well as Ariel and Mike.

God took me on a journey of trust because Mike was not quite in the same place in his faith walk as I was. So, I went to church for three years without him. God was faithful. The first verse I ever memorized was, "Trust in the Lord with all your heart and lean not on your own understanding; in all your ways submit to Him and He will make your paths straight" (Proverbs 3:5–6, NIV).

Trust was a big lesson for me, and it continues to be. I had to trust Him when He said it was time to start over. I had to trust Him when He took my son back to heaven. I had to trust Him as this journey was long and didn't look the way I had it pictured in my head. In some ways, it was better than I ever could have imagined, and in others, it was more painful than I could bear alone.

Thankfully, I had a God who would sit with me in the pit of my emotions. I learned how to grieve my son well. God showed me how my childhood narrative impacted my attraction to bad relationships, bad habits, and wrong thinking. I could start healing those parts of me that were hurt and abused and fill them with the peace and safety of healthy relationships, believing the truth that God really loved me the whole time. We can refuse to live scared and expose more light in our lives, even while walking out of darkness. Finding God doesn't mean you don't have dark or hard days. We don't live in sunshine and roses all the time. What we do have is the comfort of knowing we have a Father we can cry out to when it's too much for us to bear on our own. "I am the Lord, the God of all mankind. Is anything too hard for me?" (Jeremiah 32:27, NIV).

There isn't anything God can't handle in your broken life. Do you believe you only get one chance to make mistakes? If that were true, God would not have given me another marriage that has lasted thirty-five years. He gave me two beautiful daughters, three grandchildren (and counting!), two amazing sons-in-law, and so much new family full of love. This doesn't mean we haven't gone through much more sorrow and difficulty. It means God took me on *His* path and showed me how to break off generational dysfunction that damaged my life. He was beside me the whole time; the heart tug I always felt, even before I was a Christian, was a Holy Spirit tug, prompting me to keep moving to a better place.

My prayer these days is for our family to always be learning, listening, and following God's path. He took a broken, scared young girl and changed her heart to one of wanting to show others the beauty of healing through God's love. He will do the same for you. Just follow His plan, even when it seems impossible because God is possible. He can do the improbable things. He can move mountains and give you a mustard seed of faith like I had at the beginning of my journey. He can change the course of your life and make it new. He can lead an unchurched husband into a church with a Bible in his hand.

He will do it all because He won't stop fighting for your salvation. You are worth it, my friend.

About the Author

PHYLIS MANTELLI IS A trauma-informed coach, podcaster, and author of the book, *Unmothered: Life with a Mom Who Couldn't Love Me*. She is also an inspirational speaker at churches, retreats, conventions, Celebrate Recovery groups, and Rotary Clubs. She is currently writing her second book on lessons about how to break generational dysfunction.

She is a graduate of the Christian Communicators Conference, is a Certified LINKED Personality Coach, and is a certified trauma-informed coach with Freedom Movement.

Phylis loves helping women reach their full, God-given potential despite their trauma-filled past.

You can reach her at phylismantelli.com

CHAPTER 18

When Life Hits You Head-On

I LOVE FRIDAYS! THE last day of the workweek and the beginning of a relaxing weekend. One particular Friday evening in August 2000, I was home getting ready for a playful evening with my married daughter. We had plans for dinner and a movie.

She'd offered to drive and pick me up around five-thirty. I enjoyed her company so much that I was already having fun just being in the car with her. But we never made it to the movie that night. We were involved in a head-on auto accident six miles from the house. In the blink of an eye, a nineteen-year-old driver lost control of her car, crossed four lanes of traffic, and permanently altered our lives.

A head-on collision is one of the deadliest types of car accidents, with both vehicles typically driving at high speeds toward each other. When the crash occurs, it's like hitting a wall with no absorption of the impact. Our bodies cracked under the pressure of the violent collision.

I was knocked unconscious and awoke to the most excruciating pain I'd ever experienced. I bear eighteen inches of a cancer scar across my chest, but I have never known pain like this.

The paramedics discovered damage to my neck, a broken sternum, and a possible broken pelvis. My right hand, right kneecap, and right ankle were broken. The injury to my rotator cuff kept me from being able to raise my right arm. It took forty minutes to be removed from the car.

My daughter and I were loaded into the same ambulance because I was very direct with my request to stay close to her. I was caught between being a victim and being a mother, and I needed to know the condition of my daughter. I desperately needed to be as close to my child as possible. I thought I was dying, and I didn't want to die alone with strangers in the back of a cold, sterile ambulance. I tried to be brave as I pushed through the pain and reassured my daughter that we were going to make it. But I wasn't sure.

From the moment I regained consciousness to the moment I was placed on the X-ray table, I'd been crying out to God for my daughter and me. The emergency waiting room quickly filled with family and friends who were already praying, and the church prayer chain was activated. All those prayers caught God's ear, and He reached down into that imaging room and saw my fragile condition. My body was broken, my thoughts muddled, and the pain in my chest made it hard to breathe.

I was quite dazed from the shock of the accident as I lay on the hard X-ray table, listening to the buzz of its generator. Through the wall, I could hear the cries and screams of the other car's driver in the next room. She was reeling from her own injuries, and her fear pierced through the wall. I began to pray for her healing.

As I did, the most amazing thing took place. I could sense God's presence extending over me. Peace covered me from the top of my head to the bottom of my feet. Whatever portion of my body the imaging machine passed over instantly became warm, and the pain subsided slightly. From my neck to my feet, I felt God's protection expand over me as though He were standing at my side, passing

His hand above my body. The deep-seated fear of dying lifted off my chest, and I became so calm I could have fallen asleep.

My daughter was released from the hospital that evening. I spent three days in the hospital as doctors worked to control my pain and elevated blood pressure. Unless bones are broken, the trauma team doesn't see the grave damage done to nerves, cartilage, tendons, ligaments, and muscles. I was left with the residual fallout of soft-tissue damage. It took a few more weeks before others witnessed the impairment of a brain injury.

I returned home with an entourage of friends and family. I needed a group of people surrounding me and my two sons. My girlfriends bathed me, cooked meals, cleaned the house, and drove me to multiple doctor appointments. After enduring eighteen months of constant pain, doctor appointments, and lost wages, my spirit of gratitude for surviving the crash moved into confusion about how much longer this would last.

I cried out to God. "I would like a complete healing, please!"

In His gentle manner, God spoke to my spirit. *Be careful not to question me so much that you cross over into confusion. Back up, and trust me.*

With those words, I sat straight up in my chair as He continued to speak to my heart.

Patti, you have been thoroughly lashed by circumstances, darkness, and trouble on every side, but you have survived some of the most difficult challenges of your life! The things you have endured, though they seemed to weaken you at the time, have only made you stronger and more resolute. Rejoice in My grace. I spared your life that night.

As God spoke, a renewed resolve set in my spirit that day. I knew I'd carry the infirmities for a long time, but I also knew His grace was more than sufficient. I didn't know then, but I was about to embark on a ten-year journey through enormous obstacles as I tried to return to the life I had before the accident.

Over the span of eight years, I employed twenty-seven different doctors and therapists. I endured 416 visits to offices, rehab centers, and hospital imaging departments.

Living With a Brain Injury

As a result of one reckless driver, I was catapulted in a direction I never chose for myself . . . it was made for me. The damage to my brain is impossible to reverse. I've spent thousands of hours learning how to live with this debilitating injury. I've filled hundreds of buckets with my tears because of the injustice, the frustration, and the limitations I've had to live with. Every day, I choose to embrace a life of boundaries and make a choice to cultivate joy.

Without God's help, I would have never been able to maneuver each hurdle that lay in my path. I had a choice to make—either walk disabled in my attitude about life and all its injustice or walk with God, who is able to see me through to the other side. It took some wrestling, but I chose the latter.

As I learned to live with a permanent brain injury, I gained new coping skills that aided in my limitations. I developed new self-management skills by creating and prioritizing to-do lists, which provided measurable stability for several years. I struggled in the area of cognitive memory and attention disorder, but counseling helped me accept my limitations. Through wise counsel, I was able to stop calling myself *stupid* and see myself as the *injured* person I was.

The violent impact of the head-on auto accident caused injuries in two places inside my bony skull. First, at the site of the impact, and second, on the opposite side of the brain. The movement of the brain after the impact causes the brain to collide with the skull on the opposite side, resulting in two brain injuries. Due to the position of my head during impact, the majority of the damage is in my frontal and temporal lobes.

The area of my frontal lobe affected my ability to plan sequences of complex movements needed for fulfilling multi-step tasks. My family also noticed changes in my emotional control, motivation, impulse control, and inhibition. As I tried to adjust to my new normal, I noticed anxiety often hit when there were too many demands on me. I become anxious when my brain has to process a crowded environment, heavy traffic, or noisy children. Difficulty with reasoning and concentration makes it difficult for me to solve problems, and I become overwhelmed when asked to make a decision. I have poor judgment when it comes to people and their intentions.

The damage to my temporal lobe caused both long-term and short-term memory loss and difficulty in new learning. I also suffered a profound midline shift. A midline shift refers to a shift of brain tissue across the center line of the brain at the top of the head, separating left from right. It's associated with raised intracranial pressure, which can push the brain toward one side, which causes the midline shift. I was impacted on the right side.

This kept me from walking straight. My gait would veer to the right, causing me to hit doorways when I thought I was in the center of the doorframe. I still can't park the car straight when I turn into a parking place on the right side, but thankfully, I have no problems when I move left. It took just over two years to correct the major midline shift to a minor annoyance I have to guard for the rest of my life. I was referred to a specialized optometrist, a neuro-ophthalmologist, who studied the brain-eye connection.

He discovered visual problems in my nervous system. I still live with impaired balance issues on the right side. There is definitely a disconnect between the information my eyes bring in and how my brain processes the information.

My doctor of psychology helped me cope with the anger and anxiety caused by the accident. I would see things in my peripheral vision that weren't there. Because my depth perception was out of whack, I felt like cars were coming at me instead of being in their own lanes. I was terrified in traffic, clutching the steering wheel as though my life depended on it.

I wouldn't let anyone drive for me because I was afraid they couldn't protect me. I had to be at the wheel. Mentally, I was on high alert, ready for an ambush from another crazy driver. The stress became enmeshed in my body. When I'd see the bright red glow from someone's taillights, my heart would jump out of my chest, and I'd hit the brakes. If I heard car tires screeching on the asphalt, I would wet my pants. It took two years before I could calm down.

In March of 2002, I experienced a major breakthrough during a session with my psychiatrist. I was able to identify the debilitating fear of being behind the wheel of my car. I cried out to God. "I'm afraid, Lord. Afraid of being ambushed again!"

I knew God had saved my life the night of the crash, but I also felt like Satan got away with hurting me badly. I was watching for him to come around the corner and sucker punch me again when God wasn't looking.

The moment I made the discovery that I was allowing Satan more power in the situation than God, God broke through in a vision. He showed me right where He had been in the ambush that night. I saw the Lord at my right side traveling with me. When the other car came across the road at me, the Lord pressed in tightly to draw my head and face into His chest with His left hand, and with His right shoulder, arm, and hand, He leaned into the deadly force of the impact. It was just like a protective parent who covers a child's head with one hand while blocking and deflecting an object that comes dangerously close with the other hand. The parent absorbs the pain in place of the child. God did that for me.

Death came at me to kill me that night. God blocked the evil coming across the hood of the car. He spoke not a word . . . just raised His mighty right hand, and death had to obey. God was my weapon of defense. He absorbed *death* and released *life*; it wasn't my time to die.

God patiently healed my disjointed trust in Him to keep me from harm. The fear that gripped me so tightly for eighteen months was instantly released, and I exhaled.

Prior to the accident, I was a productive office manager for a growing company. But after three years of being unable to return to full-time work, on top of the countless mistakes I made, I left my job for the company's sake. It took me three times as long to accomplish tasks that used to be rather spontaneous.

The next four years were miserable. I tried to find a stable job with my limited skills, but I finally had to accept the fact that I wasn't going to qualify for a good job. I had to be content with piecing together several entry-level part-time jobs, which meant living paycheck to paycheck. To this present day, I'm considered unemployable in the workforce. I lost at least nine jobs because of my injuries. My inability to remember tasks, short attention span, slow pace of work, and constant knack for turning numbers around in addresses and phone numbers made it impossible to deliver my best work.

I can't operate a computer with the accuracy or pace needed in the workforce. When I look at the computer screen, I look, but I don't always see. My eye-hand coordination is impaired. I write appointments and birth dates in the wrong weeks. Comprehending time is a chore. When I look at a clock, my brain registers time one hour earlier or later than the actual time. I really have to study the face of a clock or the images on a digital dial.

Depth perception is the visual ability to perceive the world in three dimensions and the distance of an object. When this is impaired, it causes clumsiness. I spill things often, knock things over, and walk into the corner of walls. I have difficulty walking up and down stairs. The damage to my perception limits my activities. I can't stand on a balcony without the sensation that I'm going over the edge. Standing on the beach with the waves moving in and out makes me fall over. The big screen in a theater causes me great anxiety as my brain tries to take in the amplified images, so I don't go to movies.

I've learned to adapt to different layouts in public places. When I travel through a crowded mall or airport terminal, I cannot look down at the busy patterns on the floor without feeling nauseated. I've learned to look up, straight ahead, and over people's heads as I walk. When I approach a stairway, I have to pause, locate the handrail, and cling to it for dear life. Again, I can't look down at the steps because they disappear, appearing as one solid piece, like a ramp. I can't differentiate the distances between the vertical space between each step. In our fast-paced society, I definitely look like a turtle on the stairway. Don't even get me started on the struggles of using an escalator!

I'm so grateful for all the medical support I received in helping me overcome the anxiety of going out in public. Most people suffering from a brain injury become so overwhelmed and hopeless that they literally become a *recluse*. Avoiding the big world outside the front door is safer, so we create a very small and manageable world under our roof.

I cried out to God, "I'm having difficulty organizing this new lifestyle of disability. Will you help me, please?" God extended His merciful arm toward me instantly and has provided me with assistance and support every day.

I didn't get my *hope* from a prescription bottle. I received my *hope* from the Great Physician Himself. Acceptance was one of the toughest pills God asked me to swallow, but it was the one pill that brought the greatest relief to my battered mind and heart. I benefitted emotionally, mentally, and even physically once I accepted that the unpleasant reality is just as it is and cannot be changed.

- I stopped questioning and fighting the limitations for the future.

- I noticed that my body aligned itself to a more relaxed position, and recovery became possible in certain areas.

- I noticed that my anxiety was replaced with deep calmness.

- I learned how to grieve for the part of me I lost in bits and pieces and to celebrate what is left.

- I know now that life can be worth living even in the midst of pain.

I know beyond a shadow of a doubt that God saved my life that evening in August 2000. He didn't save me so I would be devoured by self-pity and anger. It's unfair what happened to me in that accident, but I'm here to testify that God's grace is more than sufficient. He asked me to glorify Him in all things.

We all want life to be fair, but it will never be, and God knows it. You and I will have moments where life hits us head on, but let's make a strong resolve that we'll never let go of God's hand. I needed Him to heal my broken bones on the X-ray table that night and guide me to all the skilled physicians and therapists who made my life manageable again. I hold onto my faith in the God of my life.

We must let Scripture guide us through the obstacle course of fear and anger. The presence of God will counsel us to grieve our losses, make a plan, and move on. Satan is the one who wants to destroy our peace and kill our testimony because he knows our testimony will influence the world. People are watching our lives. Let us live to glorify God.

About the Author

AFTER GRADUATING FROM NAZARENE Bible College in 1988 with a degree in women's studies, **Patti Davis** went on to serve as women's ministry director for several church fellowships. She's been a retreat and conference speaker for thirty-five years, as well as a lay counselor for Prison Ministries, the American Cancer Society, Celebrate Recovery, and GriefShare, and is currently the director of prayer and care at her church.

Patti is the author of the book *Hard Pressed but Not Crushed, Embracing the Lessons of Life*.

She resides in North Carolina, where she writes about her love of God while sipping coffee. Patti makes faith doable for thousands of women across this nation. Her wisdom, prophetic words, and truth telling are laced with humor. Her three adult children have blessed her with nine grandchildren and one great-grandchild.

Connect with Patti at patti-davis.com

CHAPTER 19

Getting My Voice Back

COUGHING UNTIL MY RIBS hurt, I tried to get my husband's attention. I lost my voice to a bad case of pneumonia, and it didn't return for six long weeks. Communicating your needs is tough when you have no voice. I considered throwing a tissue box at him, but my aim isn't that great. I desperately needed to either be able to talk again or have someone speak for me.

The loss of this ability hit me hard. I'd never been afraid to speak up for myself, sometimes to the point of speaking too much and without much grace. I could call someone out when necessary, and I was proud of that. Usually, though, I was speaking up on *my* behalf, protecting *my* rights, and making sure *my* needs were met.

Living six weeks without my voice taught me to treasure it. It also made me think. My voice would eventually come back, and I could speak for myself again. But what about people who, figuratively speaking, don't have a voice? Who speaks for them? People who are neglected, abused, powerless, or forgotten? That took me back to a tough chapter of my life.

I was on staff at a church, doing children's ministry. I loved it even though vocational ministry has plenty of challenges. If you know, you know. For the most part, though, things were going well. Until the day Mr. Smith walked in.

Mr. Smith was my sixth-grade teacher back in the day. Everyone loved him—until he tried to molest a classmate of mine. It should be a fireable offense, but Mr. Smith wasn't fired. He was allowed to just slink away. That's the last time I saw him until over twenty years later.

Imagine my shock when Mr. Smith showed up one day for an appointment with my boss, our lead pastor. I had no idea why he was there. He didn't attend our church. Thoughts began to race through my mind. Was he there to finally unburden himself? Was he planning to start coming to our church? I honestly wasn't sure I liked that idea. Then, I remembered how much he loved horses and how he offered pony rides at events geared toward families.

It sent me into a near panic. My staff role was children's pastor, and I couldn't stomach the thought of letting him anywhere near my little flock. They didn't have a voice, so I had to speak up for them. Finally, Mr. Smith left my boss's office, and I tore into the office, ready to do battle.

"Boss," I said. I didn't actually call him boss, but like with Mr. Smith, I'm changing his name to protect the guilty. "Boss, I don't know why that man was here, but I need to share something I know about him with you." I repeated the sordid tale I just told you. Were you horrified by my story?

My boss was not. "Lori," he said. "He has repented of that, and God has forgiven him. It seems like you are the one with the problem." I had spoken up, and I felt as though he was trying to rip my voice right out of my throat—like he was Ursula the sea witch and I was the Little Mermaid.

My speak-up side came out full force, but my grace-filled side did not. Maybe it tried, but I was already too far gone. Without much reflection, I told my boss that if Mr. Smith ever volunteered at a family or children's event at our church, I'd inform every parent what he'd done and tell them my boss knew. It felt so good! But it shouldn't have. I spoke up for the voiceless but managed to make it all about me. And I sure didn't reflect the love of Christ. I went all in on Proverbs 31:8–9 but forgot to temper that with Galatians 6:1.

It's easy to overlook those first nine verses of Proverbs 31. I love a good study on the Proverbs 31 woman, don't you? She's a boss! But those first nine verses contain directions from Lemuel's mom that speak to my heart. "Speak up for those who cannot speak for themselves; ensure justice for those being crushed. Yes, speak up for the poor and helpless, and see that they get justice" (Proverbs 31:8–9, NLT).

This sure sounds like something our Proverbs 31 woman would embrace. Between buying a field and making bedspreads, I can totally see her using her voice as a siren in defense of others and doing it well. But she's an ideal, composite version of a woman, and I'm a full-of-flaws woman. Yet God spoke to me with those verses because He truly hardwired a love of justice into my being. What He *didn't* hardwire into me was the core of Galatians 6:1–2 (NIV): "Brothers and sisters, if someone is caught in a sin, you who live by the Spirit should restore that person gently. But watch yourselves, or you also may be tempted. Carry each other's burdens, and in this way you will fulfill the law of Christ."

So, the gentle part is not hardwired into me. I'm a justice lover, and to get justice, you have to do some butt kicking ... don't you?

It is so much more satisfying than carrying the burden of the bad guys and being careful that I'm not tempted while doing it. I'm the butt-kicking, capital 'J' justice lover, remember? Then I had to ask myself, "What did my butt kicking, take-no-prisoners attitude get me when I used it with my boss?" Eventually, it led to my job being "phased out." (I'll let you decide what that's code for). I may have won the battle, but he won the war. During the fight, I admit I let it become more about being "right" than about those sweet, voiceless little children.

I realized that even though I'd done the right thing, I'd done it in the wrong way. I'd used my voice, but the people who really needed to hear from me hadn't, because I let my voice, my influence over my tiny flock, get stolen. All because I didn't temper truth with grace.

It's no coincidence that when Jesus sent his disciples out on their own, He told them in Matthew 10:16 to be "wise like snakes and gentle like doves." I spoke wisdom, but not in a gentle way. Just as God teaches us about patience by sending us circumstances that require it, He showed me how to be gentler by sending people into my life who desperately needed someone to be gentle with them. People who had lost their voices too.

My lessons from God went beyond my time in vocational ministry. Working as a paralegal in a domestic violence court brought me into contact with a lot of victims who were too frightened to use their voices. Pouring truth about the justice system on them like hot coffee would only frighten them more. I learned to be gentle with them, take things slow, and let them know that they were not at fault, no matter what their abuser told them. Some learned to trust their voices again, even in highly stressful court settings.

God also led me to jail ministry, which may seem a little odd. I figured that if I was trying to put people in jail as a private investigator, then the least I could do was help them be better people once they got out. Not very many women in the general population came to our weekly Bible studies. To get to the room where we met, I passed through the hangout spot for the ladies who weren't coming. No one spoke to me unless I spoke to them first.

One week, we made our way through security and the four locked doors, only to find that no one had shown up for Bible study. While we waited to see if anyone was running late but still coming, I started talking with the women who usually didn't say a word. There was a football game on TV, and I asked them about it. They could talk, after all!

All they needed was someone to show interest in them as people, not as a project. That bit of gentleness in showing them respect unleashed their voices. It unleashed something in me as well: a desire to keep growing in this area of using gentleness blended with justice whenever my capital 'J' justice self needed to speak.

And now, God has led me to gently work in the area of holistic church safety. It definitely takes diplomacy, and I wouldn't have been ready to step into this calling effectively had God not walked me through these other learning opportunities. My voice is powerful, and so is yours. God brings people into each of our lives whose voices are being silenced. They need us to speak up for them with both wisdom and gentleness.

Or maybe it's your voice that's been shouted down and discouraged, and you feel like your voice has been lost. Your needs are going uncommunicated. Don't throw a tissue box at anyone—just know that God is with you when you speak up *and* balance your words with grace. Fulfill the law of Christ with a gentle yet passionate voice that speaks for the ones who don't believe they can—even if that person is you.

About the Author

LORI MORRISON IS A retired private investigator who can tell you stories that would make your hair curl. She's served on church staff and has stories from that world that would also make your hair curl. She uses her experience from both to help church leaders identify and effectively deal with physical, emotional, and spiritual safety issues in their churches.

Lori has developed a training system to help mitigate safety issues. This training is essential for ministry leaders, concerned parents, pastors, and church boards. It helps everyone who wants their church to be a safe and trustworthy sanctuary for their congregations and their community.

Lori hosts an award-winning podcast called *The Unlovely Truth*, where she discusses crime against churches and crime from within churches. Her goal is to use the unlovely truths we don't always want to acknowledge to share steps churches can take to be proactive about safety. Lori also cohosts a monthly live and online book club about cold case crimes, The Cold Read.

She'd love for you to email her at lori@theunlovelytruth.com

CHAPTER 20

Purpose in Unplanned Challenges

It had been seventeen days since the lights went out; I woke up in the hospital, scared and disillusioned from a drug-induced coma, paralyzed on my left side. Emergency brain surgery was required to stop the brain bleeding, and a subsequent coma helped start the healing process. My last memory was lying on the floor with a headache, upset stomach, and a heavy left arm, with paramedics towering over me.

At just twenty-nine, and with our fifth wedding anniversary approaching, I hadn't planned on a massive hemorrhagic stroke. However, life rarely turns out as we expect. My husband, Dainis, and I learned that life changes in the blink of an eye.

My mind drifted to thoughts of my life as I knew it before the stroke. Dainis and I were happily married, living in Minnesota and working for Northwest Airlines. After being unsuccessful in family planning for several years, I decided to slow down and work for our church, thinking our root problem was busyness and stress. I was the woman who dreamed of being pregnant, the nursery, sharing the news with my husband, family, and friends, and becoming a mom. Within three weeks of my new job as the church's office manager, this "uninvited stroke" stormed into our lives.

While we can't control life's challenges, we always have a choice about how we react. God is still God on both good and not-so-good days. When difficult, unplanned challenges come, we must keep our eyes on God's best plan, not our best-laid plans. I desperately desired to be a mom, yet God chose to save my life first.

During my two-month stay, I was in three separate units of the hospital—first in the ICU, then moved to a general floor, and the last stop was the inpatient rehab center. While in rehab, no one was allowed to stay with me at night. If I wanted to roll over, I called a nurse because I still couldn't move my left side or roll over on my own. My showers consisted of sitting in a chair and letting a nurse do everything. So much for my modesty! I was the girl who would change into her gym clothes in a bathroom stall. This was almost unbearable, as were other losses of independence. After a second brain surgery to remove the malformation, preventing another brain bleed from happening, I left the hospital in a wheelchair.

I could sit up, talk, stand, and walk with assistance, although I had little movement in my left arm and hand. We went to live at my parents' home, and they cared for me while Dainis concentrated on work. Those first days were agonizing and insufferable as I pushed myself harder and harder to do the things I used to do before the stroke. I fervently wanted independence, as I could see my family was emotionally and physically exhausted. I relentlessly kept pushing myself, thinking if I persevered, life would return to normal. Thankfully, I didn't know how long the journey stretching before me would be, or I may have become discouraged or, worse, given up.

Two months after my hospital discharge, Dainis was laid off because of the aviation slowdown due to the September 11 tragedy. God was gracious by providing an opportunity for him, although it required a long-distance move to Arizona. After much prayer and heartfelt conversation, we courageously sold our first house and gave our beloved dog to a family member, said goodbye to dear friends and family, and moved cross-country.

Once we arrived in Arizona and adjusted to the temperature change, I could walk short distances with a cane while still nursing my left arm and hand. However, the hope settling in my heart that we were finally finding a sense of normalcy was dashed by a huge setback when I started having seizures resulting from the stroke. In time, I found an outstanding neurological rehab clinic, where I filled my days with therapy and seizure management, which lasted many years. I could not be left alone, and my family was always on high alert for medical emergencies. I took my treatments seriously, like a full-time job, and did all I could to regain independence and mobility. As we were successful in controlling the seizures and concentrating on therapy, I was able to take on additional things. I began working on a home therapy program, working out at the local YMCA, and became the youngest member of SilverSneakers in my early thirties.

Still desiring to be parents, we were active with Compassion International and decided to embark on an international adoption journey eight years poststroke. We wanted to give a sibling group a family, and we would finally become parents. We adopted three siblings from Colombia, South America, ages six, eight, and ten—a son and two daughters.

Through the years, our journey was full of both blessings and challenges, with more medical trials on the horizon. Parenting older adopted children was like putting together a complex puzzle. I had a strong faith and personal relationship with God before my stroke, but the challenges deepened my relationship and my dependence on God as my anchor and only source of hope and joy.

I did not realize my recovery would be lifelong, both physically and emotionally. Because we moved right after my stroke, I struggled to find my place among my peers, which, in hindsight, might have provided the emotional support my heart craved. As a young stroke survivor with a disability and an adoptive mom with children who had their own struggles, I did not easily fit back into my previous peer group.

As I became more independent and healthier, my first social opportunity was attending the women's ministry and weekly Bible study at church. God brought older women into my life to love, support, nurture, and encourage me. Serving others was an incredible way to connect, share, and heal.

Eventually, I felt God wanted me to share my life experiences with others, so I started writing my first book. However, once again, I was stopped in my tracks by a possible ovarian cancer scare. For real? That sudden and serious diagnosis resulted in a total hysterectomy and an appendectomy. Thankfully, the cyst was benign, and I was cancer free. We determined during this hysterectomy surgery that I would not have been able to successfully have biological children, so as difficult as our adoption was at times, it was part of God's plan.

The Lord touched my heart in a new way because of the possible cancer diagnosis, and I began volunteering at the cancer center, teaching patients about the power of reflection in writing. I led a Bible study for out-of-town patients at the local hotel to help with activities and positive encouragement while they were in town for their treatments. I could see that my health struggles were not in vain. God had a reason and a purpose for me inside of all of them.

I learned a lot about my healing through writing, and it is a blessing to help others write and work through their journey. We can see that every challenge is also an opportunity once we navigate through our situation's initial shock and trauma. What I didn't know when I said yes to writing was that God was opening the door to some of my newest friends, providing an avenue of support I did not know existed. Stroke recovery has always been based on physical rehabilitation, whereas a cancer journey encompasses physical and emotional recovery. I learned about grieving the loss of my past life, getting the emotional support I needed to move forward, and the blessings of having friends who understand tough medical hurdles. I felt equipped to walk alongside my fellow stroke survivors and help them on their path to a brighter tomorrow.

We are often stuck when faced with tragedies and devastation because we lack control and fear what might happen next. It seems we prefer being stuck in fear rather than persevere and move forward while afraid. God has blessed me with perseverance, and I appreciate that each challenge is an opportunity to grow and be an example to others who are on a similar path. Every trial we endure is a change to our plans and can be excruciatingly difficult, yet it is never a surprise to God and His master plan. By looking at my challenges as opportunities, I found the purpose they served and shared it with others. God doesn't always answer our prayers exactly how we want Him to, but we grow if we recognize the miracles and are grateful for all we have gleaned along the way.

Life still has its limitations for me, yet it is so full and meaningful now. As a published author and motivational speaker, I share my story of overcoming with my stroke community and have many future goals in line with helping others. I am passionate about offering encouragement and am grateful for every opportunity that presents itself. We cannot change our physical situation, but we can control our emotional reactions and what we choose as our next steps. We will have times of difficulties, as well as showers of blessings while we are on this side of heaven. God made us unique, so as a result, we handle circumstances differently when we go through unplanned, challenging times. I have found that concentrating on God's purpose for all things, good and hard, makes the painful things more acceptable.

My challenging experiences have taught me more than if my life had turned out as I originally planned and expected it to. While some days are not easy, we can only control ourselves and our faith and trust in God. At the end of our time on earth, we will meet our Creator. My goal is to hear those words written in Matthew 25:21 (NIV), "Well done, good and faithful servant!"

I encourage you to reflect on how God might turn your challenges into opportunities, allowing you to bless others. Ask God to show you how to use your painful trials for His greater purpose. When your plans don't work out the way you desire, continue persevering and looking ahead rather than getting stuck and looking back. Many courageous and impactful women in the Bible serve as examples: Mary, Martha, Ruth, Naomi, Esther, Mary Magdalene, and Mary Mother of Jesus, just to name a few. Another example, Lot's wife, is not named, and yet her story of being turned into a pillar of salt reminds us how destructive looking back can be (Genesis 19:1–38). Additionally, reflect on how you can be the friend and support system to others that your heart desires for your journey. Finally, look for the inner joy and everlasting hope that comes from knowing and depending on God, despite any tough worldly circumstances you may be walking through.

> Rejoice always, pray continually, give thanks in all circumstances;
> for this is God's will for you in Christ Jesus.
> I Thessalonians 5:16–18 (NIV)

About the Author

LORI VOBER SUFFERED A hemorrhagic stroke at age twenty-nine and then developed epilepsy from the stroke. She is a survivor, overcomer, connector, and passionate sharer of hope with others. Her message is that with the right perspective, attitude, and perseverance, we can stay unstuck and keep moving forward. Despite her difficulties, Lori and her husband, Dainis, became adoptive parents to a sibling group of three.

She published her first book, *Choices: When You Are Faced with a Challenge, What Choice Will You Make?* in March 2022 and has been connecting and encouraging others to choose to survive and thrive. Her book received the 2023 Reader's Choice Awards from The Christian Literary Awards in the categories of Christian Living and Testimonial.

Lori's journey and books can be found at lorivober.com

CHAPTER 21

Finding God's Strength in Weakness

SEVEN WORDS. "I SUBMIT to You. I am Yours." These are two simple phrases, yet they changed my life over several years as my family faced one challenge after another. If you have lived any time on this earth, you know there will be struggles, highs and lows, good and bad. It's part of being human, and, unfortunately, what I expected to be a mountaintop turned into a valley where I learned to pray, trust, and wait on God for all my needs.

It was 2015, and after living in central Florida for several years, we felt God leading us to move to be near family. It seemed everything was pointing in that direction, including our house selling within a week of being on the market. Yet, we were taking a risk because we did not have jobs. Foolish or not, we took the quick sale on the house, packed the U-Haul, and headed north to the panhandle of Florida.

A family member graciously opened their home to us while we were looking for a house and jobs. My husband and I have solid career backgrounds—mine in healthcare and his in government—so we didn't foresee any issues finding work.

Little could we imagine that our initial job hunt would be challenging. During this time, I started a job and left it rather abruptly for personal reasons, while my husband took a series of temp jobs in the slow market. It was a far cry from what we envisioned when we decided to move back "home." Often, God blessed us through friends and family who brought us food to fill our freezer and gave us money to fill the needed gaps. This went on for over a year when God, in His mercy, provided an excellent employment opportunity for my husband. But it took him to our nation's capital, where he lived in long-term hotels and rented temporary rooms while I remained behind with the kids. The days were full of "Did we hear God wrong?" "What do we do next?" "What have we done?"

I found myself wrestling with deep emotions such as anger, doubt, and frustration. Everything felt out of my control. The days were long, and there seemed no end in sight. While I was thankful my husband finally had the job we prayed for, I was unprepared to be a single parent while his job was in transition between states. There came a point when I realized there was nothing *I* could do, and it was then that I realized God had me right where He wanted me—humbled and seeking Him. Once I reached the point of desperation, all I could do was lean on Him. There was no other way.

I can be such a Type A and want things to be just so, expecting everything to go as planned. And when things didn't happen as I thought they should, it resulted in angry outbursts directed toward my children. I grew up in a home where angry words were readily spewed, and I swore never to replicate it in my family. But as the days grew into months and years, I became a person I didn't recognize as I gave way to the rage inside me.

I recall moments of heated arguments with teenagers, door slamming, and tearful phone calls to my husband, who felt powerless being so far away. There came a turning point when one of our children wrote a note on a little piece of paper that said my yelling scared him, and he hated it when I fought with his sibling. I've never forgotten the courage of that small child to be so bold to write the note and leave it on my nightstand. God used that child's honesty to humble me and made me realize I needed His help to overcome my anger and reliance on myself. It was time to fully submit myself to Him. God intended to show me that His

Way was not my way, and He wanted my heart. I had lost my way and needed to get back to the feet of the Savior. I was at a loss for what to do, but He caringly showed me the next steps.

During those dark days, I rose early to pray, journal, and read the Word of God. As I journaled my prayers one morning, I ended it with, "I give, Lord. I submit it to You. I am Yours. I don't understand what is happening in our lives, but I trust You." I kneeled at the chair and said again, "I submit to You. I am Yours." Little did I know this mantra would go on for months. There was almost a physical restraint in my spirit that God would not allow me to rise from that chair until I bent the knee to His will and submitted to His ways. Over and over again. Rinse and repeat. Read the Word. Journal. Kneel at the chair. "I submit to You. I am Yours." And then He released me to start the day. But it wasn't easy, as I still struggled with anger and felt so alone. I realized I could not control my anger and needed to proactively address this issue in my life.

I heard that praying the Word of God was one sure way to pray for His will. Based on a teaching, I decided to look up Scriptures about anger in the Bible. I typed several pages of sobering verses about anger, stapled them together, and began to pray them repeatedly over my life and my words.

I prayed Scriptures, such as Proverbs 15:1 (NIV). "A gentle answer turns away wrath, but a harsh word stirs up anger." I'd pray, "Lord, forgive me for my harsh words towards my children. Help me have a gentle answer when I speak." Or Ecclesiastes 7:9 (HCSB): "Don't let your spirit rush to be angry, for anger abides in the heart of fools." Another prayer. "Lord, don't let me rush to anger. Please help me to be patient. I don't want to have the heart of a fool." I kept this list close at hand to pray frequently over my struggle with anger.

I knew I could not overcome this on my own. I needed a change of heart that could only come from God and the Holy Spirit working in me. As I prayed those verses continually, God, slowly but surely, softened my heart and restrained my tongue. His peace that passes all understanding took root in my soul, replacing my anxious thoughts (Philippians 4:6–7). Those pages became worn with fingerprints and tears as they became my map to a changed heart.

Throughout these years, gratitude also became a lifeline. God reminded me that, like the Israelites in the Old Testament, I quickly forgot what He had done in my life and for our family. He has a long track record of proving Himself faithful to me and my family, but I was so focused on our circumstances and trying to figure out the next steps that I forgot His faithfulness. Inspired by Ann Voskamp's book, *One Thousand Gifts*, I began to journal my blessings, memories of His faithfulness in the past, and the unseen answers ahead of us. Every day before my husband landed that job, I entered a line in my gratitude journal. "Thank you for my husband's job." Hebrews 11:1(NET) reminds us, "Now faith is being sure of what we hope for, being convinced of what we do not see." I knew in my head that God would provide, but I needed my heart to catch up to that belief. I had to boss it around and tell my soul to be thankful for what was not yet.

While I will always continue learning, God used those years of heartache, disappointment, and uncertainty to help me overcome fear, doubt, and anger. He helped me overcome my tendency to rely on myself or others for joy. Only God knows what is ahead, but I know He has good plans for me. I can trust Him with whatever He puts in my path, good or bad. God's blessing continued to pour out on us as my husband's job miraculously transferred him back home, and doors opened for me in ways I never imagined. This time in the valley taught me that God is faithful, and His steadfast love endures forever.

After this season, I often thought about the story in Luke 22:31–32 where Jesus told Peter that Satan wanted to sift the disciples like wheat, and He prayed Peter's faith would not fail. I believe I was sifted like wheat for a season, but it strengthened my faith and would serve a purpose to inspire others. We know that all things work together for good for those who love the Lord (Romans 8:28), and ultimately, God drew me closer to Himself, knowing that His power is made perfect in my weakness (2 Corinthians 12:9).

Regardless of what you are facing, turn your face toward Him, submit to His ways, and thank Him in all things—including those you have not received yet but know to align with His Word and His Will. Revelation 12:11 tells us that our testimony is powerful. I pray this testimony will serve as a reminder that in Christ, we can overcome every obstacle that comes our way.

About the Author

DARCY HICKS WRITES AND speaks after hours from her day job as a nursing executive. She writes to encourage and strengthen people on their faith journey to know and love God. Darcy inspires hope through sharing the Word of God.

She is a Southern transplant living near the white, sandy beaches of Northwest Florida. She loves spending time with her husband, Terry, and their children. She is involved in her local church, serves in women's ministry, and is active in her community as a member of a Rotary club.

Connect with Darcy at darcyhicks.com

CHAPTER 22

My Journey on the Yellow Brick Road

THE SOUND OF MY footsteps on the wooden planks of the old Potter's Bridge echoed as I prayed ...

"Lord, I'm scared. So much in my life has changed. I am desperate to find a new path. Show me where You want me to go."

I signed the papers for my divorce after being married for twenty-four years. I didn't have health insurance or a retirement account. The economy was brutal to my home decorating business, and I was on the verge of losing my house. My thoughts were in panic mode.

As I opened the door to my Chevy Astro van, which had traveled over 177,000 miles, I heard the question: *Do you trust me?* It wasn't audible, but my heart heard it.

I picked up *The Indianapolis Star's* classified section. Most jobs required a college degree, but I surrendered mine when I was married after my freshman year of college.

The newspaper fell to the floor and opened to an ad for a salesperson opening at Don Hinds Ford. I did have twenty-six years in sales, but I knew nothing about cars or trucks and never worked with men. The ad said, "Training. Demo vehicle. Health Insurance. 401(k)."

Opening my Bible, the first Scripture I read was Habakkuk 1:5 (NIV): " Look [...] and be utterly amazed. For I am going to do something in your days that you would not believe, even if you were told."

The arguing with God began. "I am forty-eight years old. I know nothing about cars and trucks. I have never worked with men."

Do you trust me?

That night, I wrestled with the blanket and the thought of calling the dealership and asking for an interview. I told no one about what happened at Potter's Bridge.

Making the call to the sales manager and walking into the showroom were two of the scariest moments of my life. While I told the sales manager I had never worked with men and knew nothing about cars and trucks, he saw twenty-six years of sales experience. He told me to show up the next Monday for training.

What was I thinking? This made no sense.

Do you trust me?

I walked out of that showroom, the only one wearing pink, with unfriendly stares from the car guys. I entered a man's world, even worse, a car guy's world. Fear gripped every part of my being. My family and friends would, for sure, think I lost my ever-loving mind. Perhaps I had lost my mind, thinking I could start this new venture at forty-eight years old.

For weeks, I slept with training manuals, learning about gear ratios, diesel engines, and other car and truck facts I never imagined having to know. Even more challenging was the not-so-friendly atmosphere in a world where women were not welcome.

No one was more surprised than I that I was becoming quite the car and truck salesperson. In a sales meeting, my sales manager said he had no idea what I was doing to sell so many vehicles, but he didn't think I knew either. He was right.

I kept to myself in my closet-like office unless I was out on the car lot, literally pounding the pavement, often running into a customer. Most were surprised to find a lady salesperson and felt somewhat at ease dealing with one. I tried my best to make buying a car fun.

Three months into finding myself on a yellow brick road, I discovered I had a brain and heart, but most of all, courage. I was not only successful at selling cars and trucks, but the guys began to accept me.

One guy, Jay, was particularly gruff, and I was terrified of him. He walked into my office and sat down. My heart raced as he began to talk. "Church Lady (his not so endearing name for me), you have gumption. I'm going to teach you this business." It was a good thing I was sitting down, or I would have fainted on the hard tile floor.

He sat with me and drank coffee every morning, mostly explaining the parts and workings of trucks. I became the truck lady. He had quite the ability to use the F-bomb fluently as a verb, noun, pronoun, conjunction, and adverb. This church lady just smiled. *He may teach me the fine art of selling trucks but never the colorful language of a car guy.*

One morning, two years into finding success in the car business, Jay said to me, "Church Lady, you need to send a column to the *Noblesville Daily Ledger*. They are asking for guest columnists."

I quickly reminded him I didn't finish college, let alone have a journalism degree.

"You have a way with words. I have to sit here and listen to you tell stories for hours every day. You know how to tell a story."

I will forever hear his next words. "I dare you!"

My fingers tapped away on the keyboard, putting together my thoughts about my journey on the yellow brick road to a car dealership. In writing my story, I relived the feelings of fear that gripped me financially, but with my leap of faith, I found I had a brain, a heart, and most of all, courage.

Do you trust me?

I answered with a huge leap of faith. At the age of forty-eight, I found I could not only fly, but I could soar, and I had the "Salesperson of the Year" plaque to prove it! But most of all, I knew what Habakkuk 1:5 meant. I would have never believed what God would do ... even if He told me.

What happened after the column was submitted and published was even more of a God appointment. My friends called and said, "I didn't know you could write." Neither did I.

A few days after the column was published, the editor called and asked if I would write another column. I wrote about the places you will go if you leave the baggage behind. It told of forgiving my ex-husband after his betrayal.

It was a hot day in August, and I was in the middle of a car deal when my phone rang. It was the newspaper's editor. She wanted to see me in her office. What could she want to see me about?

"Janet, we have had quite the response to your writings. Would you be a weekly columnist for us?"

The Truck Lady became a newspaper columnist with a column titled, From the Hart. Hart was my maiden name. My column made people laugh and cry, but most of all, it made them think. They could relate to so much of what I wrote. I loved telling stories and was amazed that people thought I had a gift for writing.

This leap of faith brought me to a new Promised Land. I was now a published writer.

Oh my goodness, God sure was writing an amazing story as He held my pen, but there was another story I didn't know He was writing: a love story for me. He wasn't finished.

Over the years, I dabbled in dating. I was skeptical and afraid. I was hurt to the most tender part of my heart, and a protective barrier grew over the years. Dating is not for the faint of heart.

Great expectations can lead to great disappointments. Let's just say I could write a short book about dating, and you would not believe some of the stories. I call them dabbling disasters. Enough said.

I've always written in my Bible, underlining Scriptures that spoke to me and writing the date when I read them. I encountered Isaiah 43:18–19 (NIV): "Forget the former things; do not dwell on the past. See, I am doing a new thing! Now it springs up; do you not perceive it? I am making a way in the wilderness and streams in the wasteland."

I wrote beside that verse with the date, 10/8/2012: "We must let go of the past and take hold of God's plan for our future!"

What in my past did I need to let go of? I asked God to show me. What fear caused me to hold back on moving into the future? Time and prayer eventually showed me. *Help me, Lord, to let go.*

It was late August 2013 when I walked through the dealership's waiting room. Sitting in a leather chair and reading a book was a man I had become acquainted with over the years. I knew some of his story. He was a retired superintendent from Hamilton Southeastern Schools. He had two sons, and his wife passed away in 2012 after her battle with cancer. We chatted whenever he brought his car in for service. He sat in the sales waiting room where it was quiet, unless he ran into this chatty sales lady.

"Hello Chuck, how is your day going?"

He looked up from the book he was reading. He had the sweetest smile. "Janet, it's a good day. Just getting the oil changed."

We exchanged news about our lives, and as I turned to continue walking out to the service area, I heard him say, "Janet, if you are not seeing anyone, could I take you to lunch or dinner sometime?"

I turned around and said, "Yes." I had sworn off dating. No way. I was done with hoping to find love. Why did I say yes so quickly? What was I thinking? Well, what would one lunch date ever lead to?

One lunch led to one dinner that led to quite the love story. Three weeks after we started dating, Chuck told me he was falling in love with me. I told him I thought we were going in the same direction, but he was on a mountain bike, and I was on a tricycle. If he would slow down, I would catch up.

The next day, I fell while out shopping and severely sprained my ankle. He showed up at the hospital and strolled into the treatment room, saying the nurse told him my husband could come in to be with me. At that moment, I knew I had "fallen" in love with Chuck Leonard. Schmaltzy huh?

We were married six months later. We are the vintage people's version of *The Big Bang Theory*. Chuck has his doctorate in education and well, I'm the Truck Lady.

In 2020, when COVID hit and put us in the Twilight Zone, I retired. My husband said, "Honey, now it's time to write your book." So, I did.

At the age of sixty-six, I published my first book, *When the Hart Speaks: Whimsy and Wisdom from the Little House on the Alley*. Now, I am writing book number two, and I'm speaking at churches, women's events, and book clubs.

Overcoming my fear of starting a new life at forty-eight has been an unbelievable blessing. All those many years ago, God told me in Habakkuk 1:5 (NIV), "For I am going to do something in your days that you would not believe, even if you were told."

Fear, humiliation, and anger were turned into such a beautiful life full of blessings beyond what I could have ever prayed for.

When I write, I often share my struggles but also my faith and how God is a God of redemption. He can do so much more than we could ever imagine. God held my pen and wrote a beautiful story. There will be more chapters to write as I trust God.

I pray my words glorify who God can be in your life when you have no choice but to start over with a leap of faith. If you trust Him, God will take you to places you never imagined.

Whenever I walk on the wooden planks in that old, covered bridge, I hear an echo of God's promises. *See, Janet, I did something that, had I told you, you would not have believed...but you trusted Me.*

Blessed is she who has believed that the Lord would fulfill his
promises to her!

Luke 1:45 (NIV)

About the Author

JANET HART LEONARD IS a newspaper columnist, author, and speaker. Nothing in her life has gone as planned, but God has written an amazing story as He's held her pen.

Janet shares her life and pieces of her heart as she writes to her readers. She can often be found at one of her local coffee shops or cafes, where everyone knows her name, or she becomes the new friend you always wanted.

If you visit Janet at her home, you'll likely find her tending to her flower garden or reading on her back porch. She might even offer you a slice of her homemade chocolate cream pie, inviting you to sit and chat for a while.

Janet has grown up and grown into her older years, all the while living on the same street for almost seven decades. She shares her century-old home with her Prince Charles, whom she found in the waiting room where she sold cars and trucks. Their love story is worthy of the plot of a Hallmark movie.

You can read about her journey on her yellow brick road in her book, *When the Hart Speaks: Whimsy and Wisdom from the Little House on the Alley.*

Connect with Janet:

Website: janethartleonard.com
Facebook: Janet Hart Leonard

CHAPTER 23

Forged Through the Fire

AN UNLIKELY JOURNEY TO JOY

A CHORUS SWIRLED AROUND me as I looked at the words on the screen but couldn't sing them. Those around me raised their hands and lifted their voices to declare that God's love never fails. But all I could do was stand and stare.

My body was in the third row of the sanctuary at church. But my soul was numb with pain, and my spirit felt disconnected from its Maker. Tears streamed down my face, and a knot twisted in my stomach. How could I sing "Your Love Never Fails" when it felt like God *had* failed me? Day after day, week after week, I fell to my knees in prayer, desperate for God's healing touch. But day after day, week after week, I fell deeper into the darkness.

My soul was weak and weary. Worst-case scenarios taunted my mind like a bully on the playground—relentless in spinning the merry-go-round faster and faster despite my pleas to get off the ride. Nauseous and gasping for air, I could never quite catch my breath. The sleepless nights supplied the perfect conduit for my fears to pillage their way to the surface and escape through the vent of rage. The tiniest drop of stress set the pot of my emotions boiling over, burning those in range of my anxious inferno.

As I stood in church that chilly Sunday morning, fully aware of my fragile existence, I wondered if the lyrics of the chorus were true. Does joy really come in the morning after a night of pain? I knew this song was based on Psalm 30:5, but my mind, body, and soul could not rest in the hope this Scripture existed to provide. Night after night, I wept. And morning after morning, the daybreak illuminated the agonizing reality that joy had, once again, not come.

Have you ever been there, friend? Desperate to experience the joy of the Lord but painstakingly numb to its effects? It's such a cold and relentless prison, isn't it?

What is Joy?

Joy. It may be one of the most petite words in the English language, but it holds one of the most profound meanings—and it's often misunderstood.

What comes to mind when you hear the word *joy*?

Walking down the aisle on your wedding day? Slipping your toes into the warm sand on the beach? Seeing the twinkle in your children's eyes as they open gifts on Christmas morning? Maybe it's the way the sun streams through your window in the morning or the glorious colors of the sky on your evening walk. Perhaps it's waking up refreshed after a good night of sleep.

Joy is most often associated with feelings of happiness, bliss, delight, wonder, serenity, and pleasure. And while interchanging the words joy and happiness is not altogether wrong, happiness is a sore underrepresentation of the depth of godly joy. Happiness is a situational feeling that evaporates the moment life throws us a curveball. But joy is a fruit of God's Spirit that is forged and expanded through the fiercest fires of this life.

> Consider it pure joy, my brothers and sisters, whenever you face
> trials of many kinds, because you know that the testing of your

faith produces perseverance. Let perseverance finish its work so
that you may be mature and complete, not lacking anything.

James 1:2–4 (NIV)

Now, I'm going out on a limb here to wager that situations involving *trials, tests, trouble, or pressure* didn't swing to the forefront of your mind as you pondered what joy feels like. Yeah, me neither.

If you've known the God of the Bible for any length of time, you've likely discovered He has a knack for flipping cultural norms on their head. In God's upside-down kingdom, the last will be first (Matthew 20:16), the least will be the greatest (Matthew 23:11, Luke 9:48), and joy can be found through suffering (James 1:2–4). If there was ever a verse to summarize the conflict that arises within me from this topsy-turvy way of thinking, it's Isaiah 55:8: "'For My thoughts are not your thoughts, Nor are your ways My ways,' says the Lord."

And all God's people said, "Amen!"

Considering it "pure joy" to go through trials sounds impossible, doesn't it? But many of us have experienced this phenomenon firsthand, and it's truly remarkable. We've also had to overcome some misconceptions about the genuine essence of biblical joy.

Perhaps you've been taught having joy means feeling happy and satisfied as you sweep your problems under the rug and hide behind the "I'm fine! Everything's good. Nothing to complain about!" mask. Maybe joy has been the spiritual Band-Aid others have tried to stick on your pain as they attempt to console you with all-too-common and oh-so-irritating pep talk: "Don't worry, it's all going to be okay! Just keep praying and stay positive. God's got this!"

Throughout my life, I've been both the recipient and the reciter of these well-intended platitudes. The problem with these silver-lined statements, other than negating our pain, is that they miss a crucial lesson that our trials teach us: *the power of perseverance.*

When I was in the depths of anxiety and depression as a young mom, I considered it anything but pure joy to be walking this debilitating road. I felt lost in my faith, confused about my identity, and overwhelmed by my steady decline into despair. It just didn't make sense. And no collection of Christian Hallmark sentiments helped me feel better or moved me toward healing.

So, how did I grab hold of God's command to consider it pure joy to face trials of many kinds?

By allowing the testing of my faith to develop perseverance.

There is No Easy Button

Were you a CliffsNotes reader in school? Or maybe, like me, you watched the made-for-TV movie instead of reading the book? Many of us are on a constant hunt for an "easy button," especially when it comes to avoiding assignments we don't want to do.

Unfortunately, for you and me both, there is no easy button to growing our character. It's a messy, painful, wonderful, and terrible process that takes time and requires the testing of our faith. *New York Times* best-selling author, Matthew Kelly, gives a profound reflection on character development in his thoughtful book, *Life Is Messy*:

> Character can be acquired intentionally, by proactively developing habits of the heart, mind, body and soul. It can also be acquired passively by enduring life's inconveniences, difficulties, and un-avoidable suffering. But there are no shortcuts. You cannot hack your way to character. It is the greatest investment you can make in yourself.[1]

---

1. Matthew Kelly, *Life is Messy* (Blue Sparrow Publishing, 2021), 136–7.

It's hard to pinpoint what I did to persevere through my trials of anxiety and depression. I just know I showed up and kept showing up. I joined a mom's group at my church and slowly began to let myself be known, warts and all. I went to therapy every week and slowly learned how to reframe my mindset. I attended a rapid symptoms reduction class through my hospital and slowly learned coping techniques for living with anxiety and depression. I joined an intensive course on overcoming trauma and slowly made peace with things that were out of my control while learning to take responsibility for what was within my control. And I slowly overcame my fear of the side effects of antidepressants and gave myself permission to begin taking medication for my mental illness.

I persevered under pressure and came out more refined in my character.

As I sit with this passage of Scripture in James, I see how God clarified my understanding of joy. James is not saying that joy comes from suffering itself. Trials without hope are a highway into endless darkness and despair. James is also not saying that having the joy of the Lord means we're constantly giddy with excitement, carrying around handfuls of confetti to throw in the air as we walk through the fiery furnace.

James is saying we can place our trust in God to walk with us *through* our trials. We can hold onto the hope that joy, maturity, and a more complete understanding of God's character and love are waiting for us on the other side of our suffering—should we choose to persevere. The late Timothy Keller beautifully articulates this idea in his book, *Walking with God through Pain and Suffering*:

> Christianity teaches that, contra fatalism, suffering is overwhelming; contra Buddhism, suffering is real; contra karma, suffering is often unfair; but contra secularism, suffering is meaningful. There is a purpose to it, and if faced rightly, it can drive us like a nail deep into the love of God and into more stability and spiritual power than you can imagine.[2]

---

2. Timothy Keller, *Walking with God Through Pain and Suffering* (Penguin Books, 2015), 30.

The Juxtaposition of Joy

It's taken time and distance from the eye of the storm, but I can look back and see how the path of pain can be a route to joy and growth.

As a survivor of childhood trauma, I am more sensitive to the suffering and shortcomings of others. As a Christian woman who battles the beasts of generalized anxiety disorder and clinical depression, I am more thoughtful in how I speak about mental illness and suicide. As someone who has lived with chronic pain for almost twenty years, I am more patient with those who require more assistance and time to get around. By pressing on through the storm, I have gained knowledge and depth of insight (Phil 1:9) that I would not have gained otherwise.

Joy became real for me when I experienced the great exchange: my captivity for His freedom, my ashes for His beauty, and my destruction for His restoration (Isa 61). I have found joy in realizing God was true to His word in never leaving me or forsaking me (Heb 13:5). Joy has sprouted from seeing God use what I've learned through my own painful experiences to help someone else navigate theirs (2 Cor 1:3–5).

The truest source of joy comes from the knowledge and reality that Jesus paid the price for my sins and made a way for me to be reconciled to God the Father. And, as James says, I can consider it pure joy to face trials of many kinds because Jesus faced trials of many kinds. I can consider it pure joy when my faith is tested because Jesus was tested too. I can consider all of this pure joy because of the power of perseverance.

Like the cross Jesus endured for our salvation, some of the best gifts come through suffering.

But the hardest part is the waiting, the time in between when the storm ends and when we receive the promised prize once we reach the shore again. I relate to the honest words of one of my favorite authors, Michele Cushatt, in her book *A Faith That Will Not Fail*:

I've never been much good at waiting. When I want something, I want it sooner than later ... I want my children to be mature and faithful today, and my relationships to be what God designed them to be right now. I want to skip over the uncomfortable process and get to the satisfying results. But I too easily forget: the struggle now is part of the glory later.[3]

Dear one, joy is not the elimination of trials. It is the fruit that comes from persevering *through* our trials. Joy is found in choosing to have hope beyond our circumstances. It is recalling the times God has been faithful before and choosing to believe He will be faithful again. Through the storm, I have come to believe the lyrics of that song I couldn't sing that chilly Sunday morning all those years ago: His love, indeed, never fails. And though pain may last for many, many nights, I choose to believe His joy will come in the morning. I pray you will choose to believe it too.

---

3. Michele Cushatt, *A Faith That Will Not Fail: 10 Practices to Build Up Your Faith When Your World Is Falling Apart* (Zondervan, 2023), 241–2.

About the Author

HAVE YOU EVER FELT as though you're simultaneously 'too much' and 'not enough'? **Andrea Nyberg** understands that struggle intimately.

As a Christian author and speaker, she is dedicated to helping you reframe those feelings and discover true freedom in your faith, identity, and mental health.

Andrea's honest, heartfelt approach to challenging topics resonates deeply with audiences. She creates a safe space where pain and hope can coexist, making her a highly sought-after speaker for groups ready to embrace authentic growth.

Rooted in Scripture's promises, Andrea will guide you through the transformative journey of exchanging your fears for God's liberating freedom. Whether you're seeking personal growth or looking for an impactful speaker for your women's group or student event, Andrea offers valuable insights and practical tools.

With a master's degree in educational leadership from Gateway Seminary and in-progress certification as a faith-based, trauma-informed Freedom Coach, Andrea brings both expertise and compassion to her work.

Connect with her at AndreaMNyberg.com

CHAPTER 24

Moving Past Constant Distress

CONSTANT DISTRESS. THAT IS the phrase that describes my teenage years. There was never safety, and I never felt worthy. I tried hard to be someone people considered worthy, but I was a fraud. I knew nothing about authenticity because there was always fear, panic, and anger in my heart. I longed to be at peace, just as I perceived others to be.

I grew up in an ordinary Christian family. Hot summers working on the farm with the family, going to church every service, attending school, and playing basketball throughout the school year was a typical life for everyone in my sweet little town of about one hundred people. Life was routine, with little excitement or drama, until it changed drastically for me. From the age of fourteen to seventeen, I was sexually molested by a person I had known all my life. They told me that if I said anything, my family would be hurt—physically and emotionally—and it would be because of me. I believed that to be true, but I also thought my family would no longer want me if they knew. I didn't want to hurt people in my family; I loved them and wanted to be loved by them. So, I never told anyone.

Continuing with my life, I attended college, played basketball, married, and had three precious children. However, neither I nor my husband were emotionally equipped to have a healthy marriage. We were both damaged and broken. Unfortunately, we went through a devastating divorce because I could see that my children were being raised in a toxic environment. I asked my husband to go to counseling with me, but he refused. Eventually, I sought counseling to see what was wrong with me.

In my mid-thirties, I started psychotherapy. I also started spending a lot of time in the Bible. Reading God's Word taught me that my self-esteem and worth came from Christ, not myself or the world. I began to long to know more about the gospel, and the more time I spent seeking, the more I could see the truth. And the more I could see the truth, my life changed. The changes were challenging (e.g., divorce, single parenting, job changes, relationship changes). Now, I look back and see God's hand shaping and growing me into what He wanted me to be all along. This period of counseling and time spent with God finally allowed me the freedom to tell the truth.

The truth that will set you free is a Bible verse from John 8:32 (KJV), which says, "And ye shall know the truth, and the truth shall make you free." In this verse, Jesus Christ speaks to a group of Jews who believe He is the Messiah. John 8 explores the identity and authority of Christ and how they relate to freedom, forgiveness, sin, and judgment. Verses 31–47 focus on what it means to be free, happy, and saved. But after my divorce, it was a verse that allowed me to heal from my brokenness—a moment to say aloud that the truth meant freedom and forgiveness.

At forty, after feeling unloved and unlovable for most of my life, I finally shared my experience, only to discover it had happened to another family member. Some of my family members were angry with me, while others were disappointed in both me and the offender. A few of them believed I lied. None of them told me it wasn't my fault and that I would be okay. It was never talked about again except between the other victim and me.

Keep in mind I was raised in a Christian family. I now understand that my family was not emotionally equipped to handle the trauma that occurred. Unlike me, they had never experienced trauma in this way. Like me, they didn't know what to do with the emotions.

To heap burning coals onto trauma, I was often compared to siblings by family and friends. This added to the constant anger, sadness, and unworthiness that nagged at my heart for years. I felt I never measured up. As an adult, I acted out in ways that were unbecoming of someone who professed to be a Christian. I didn't know what depression and anxiety were. But I came to realize I had been experiencing both for most of my life.

Christ strengthened me and grew my faith in unexpected ways. He placed people in my path, and I knew He wanted me to minister and help them. If this trauma had never happened to me, I would not have known what to say or do. He also gave me mentors to help me grow spiritually. The struggle to grow and shape my life to be more Christlike was hard, but I now see how it glorifies Him. My life is not perfect by any means, but it is better. God walks with me through tough times even now. However, the difference between then and now is that I lean into Him and don't try to do things my way or hide from Him and everyone else. I strive to have a content relationship with Him and to grow in the ways He wants me to.

Interestingly, or maybe the correct word is ironically, I went to school to learn to be a counselor for effective service. This was long before I went to counseling myself. God was leading the way before I knew it was the way I was to follow. I am a licensed professional counselor-supervisor with a Ph.D. in general psychology. My career as a counselor allows me to help others and helps me continue to grow. When I listen to clients talk about being molested and how they feel—the guilt, fear, hate, anger, and sadness—I can relate to them because I have felt every one of those emotions. I understand that sexual abuse doesn't define me, and this part of my life, and my client's, is not my fault or theirs. Someone else forced behavior on us that was not of our doing.

When a client comes to see me to discuss this subject, my mind goes back to that sweet Bible verse. "And ye shall know the truth, and the truth shall make you free" (John 8:32, KJV).

Jesus loved me through that dark time. Even though my mind could not comprehend that anyone could love me, He loved and still loves me. I know that now, but I didn't know it until He brought healing through counseling and drawing close to Him in His Word. It is my great honor to help others who have gone through similar trauma and help them find peace amid their storms.

If you are in a situation that doesn't feel right, you feel trapped, and you are being sexually abused, reach out to someone who can help you now; this is not your issue. It is the perpetrator's issue. Women in their 70s and 80s come to me and, for the first time, confess that they were abused. They felt isolated, alone, depressed, and anxious all their life. You are caught up in someone else's sin, so tell someone now. If you don't know whom you can trust, I promise you that you can trust God. Talk to Him, cry out to Him, and He will show you who you can trust with the information and help you navigate out of your situation.

If you are made aware of a child who is being sexually abused, please do something immediately to make sure they are safe. Helping a traumatized child heal through Christ involves reminding them that God cares for and understands their suffering, and that one day, if they have received Christ, all the pain will end.

Some ways to help a child who has experienced trauma include:

Incorporate Christian Practices into Daily Routines

This includes family worship, prayer at meal times, and reading Scripture together. Consistency and routine help children feel secure and build trust and healing.

Ask for God's Help

Ask God to help you acknowledge and accept what you are becoming aware of. You can also express your feelings honestly to God and share them with others struggling with similar issues.

Remember God's Promises

God promises to protect and flourish his children, even amid trauma healing. This promise helps children remember the darkness, tears, and suffering will eventually end.

The hills and valleys I have walked through and still walk through are filled with God's grace to help me mature and grow. He equips me to walk the path He designed for me. I increasingly realize that my job is to love others going through difficult times and show them Christ. Each day, He allows me to speak, write, sing, counsel, and teach others about how to receive Christ as their personal Savior. Clients call and make appointments, or God has divine appointments I don't see coming. He has also given me a group of ladies who have been hurt due to sexual trauma to meet with once a week. The group is called "Courage to Heal," which is precisely what it takes .... courage.

God has an excellent plan for your life, too. Jeremiah 29:11 (NIV) says, "'For I know the plans I have for you,' declares the Lord, 'plans to prosper you and not to harm you, plans to give you hope and a future.'"

If you are a sexual abuse survivor, I urge you to seek counseling and find someone who can help you read and study the Bible. If you are helping someone else navigate sexual abuse, I encourage you to help them find Jesus as their personal Savior to find hope and healing. Seek therapy with a counselor or talk to a friend, mentor, or pastor. They are all great options. Seeking Christ is a must for anyone suffering from this or any other abuse.

Here is the national hotline if you need to reach out now: 1-800-656-4673.
There is help. Look deep down inside yourself and see the person Jesus sees who has worth, beauty, and strength.

About the Author

DR. GAYLA CAMPBELL IS a frequent speaker, writer, BMI songwriter, and counselor. Her passion is to help others who are in emotional pain. Her warmth, compassion, and humor are evident to all who read her writings or hear her speak. She is a two-time winner of the International Impact Book Award and the Christian Literary Award for her book, *Pursuing God's Heart.*

She has also written *Healing Hurts Curriculum, Finding Joy after Divorce,* and *An Inside View of Grief.*

She and her husband, Gary, provide concerts and speaking engagements through their nonprofit company G&G Ministries.

You may reach them at gandgministries3@gmail.com

CHAPTER 25

When Tragedy Strikes

"SUZANNE, YOU HAVE A detached retina in your right eye and need surgery either this evening or first thing tomorrow morning." My whole world came crashing down in a moment. This was supposed to be a routine eye appointment, but it became a critical care situation that left me breathless. I wish I could tell you the first reaction in my mind and heart was to talk to Jesus. Instead, every fearful thought possible crept into my mind. I left the office with my eight-year-old daughter, Shelby, in complete shock.

The next morning, my husband, Logan, and I took Shelby with us to the retinal institute, where I thought I was having surgery. The kind staff started the exam, and I noticed there was more to this exam than the day before. The specialist entered the room with such a warm demeanor. Two ladies followed behind him. They chatted with us briefly and then lured Shelby out of the room to get some candy down the hall, closing the door behind them.

The doctor told me I would not be having surgery that day. I felt a fleeting moment of relief. He went on to share he had a working diagnosis that needed to be confirmed by another eye specialist. He said, "I am pretty certain you have a choroidal malignant melanoma."

A what? I didn't know eye cancer existed.

He told me I needed to see an ocular oncologist to confirm the diagnosis and referred me to the best specialist in the state. I was scheduled to meet the ocular oncologist nine days later. The moment I left the retinal institute building, I erupted into tears. Horrible scenarios entered my mind, even though I didn't know yet what I was facing. I had no idea where to start processing the news, but I knew I had to start praying for my healing right away, despite not being able to shake the numbness I felt.

The big appointment day rolled around quickly. After four hours of photographs, an ultrasound, various eye tests, and lots of waiting, I met the ocular oncologist, who confirmed the diagnosis: there was a choroidal malignant melanoma in my right eye. I was hoping he would tell me nothing was there and that whatever was found at the retinal institute was gone. It's what I prayed for, but it was not the case.

The doctor told me I could have brachytherapy (radiation delivered through a small plaque) to treat the tumor. He shared that only one in six million receive this diagnosis and removing the eye would not affect the risk of metastasis. I was thirty-six years old and honestly didn't even know what metastasis meant. I quickly learned ocular melanoma is an aggressive cancer with a risk of metastasis primarily to the liver and other vital organs. I opted to have the tumor biopsied during the plaque insertion surgery to know the metastatic risk for my body.

I could not bear the weight of all this by myself. Wonderful family members were by my side and friends and church family were lifting me up in prayer, but it was not enough to ease the mental and emotional toll that set in. I grieved, knowing I would never be the same again after this life-altering diagnosis.

I dug into the Word for verses on healing and peace. I wept ... a lot. I did not understand but knew I could not walk through this day in and day out without my Heavenly Father. It didn't take me long to figure out I needed to seek Him.

The walk I maintained with the Lord in previous years was due for an overhaul. Being on the worship team at church and sleepily reading my morning devotion wasn't enough. I started to read the Word, pray the Word, and trust Him with my whole heart. I knew this was what I was supposed to do as a Christian, but I'd allowed my busy, working mom life to get in the way of seeking the Lord on a daily basis.

The rest of the summer was mostly a blur. My body stayed in a complete state of exhaustion during the seven days of plaque radiation. My family never told me how gruesome I looked or how difficult it was for them to see my body, heart, and soul battling cancer when I was at my worst. I remember praying with my mom and talking to the Lord every day. These were not rehearsed prayers. I thanked my Heavenly Father for helping eye doctors find the problem so it could be treated and asked Him for physical and mental strength. I felt His loving presence even through utter exhaustion.

Just over a month after the radiation plaque was removed, I learned the biopsy showed a class 2 tumor, which means the greatest risk of metastasis (72 percent) within five years. To God be the glory, I am celebrating six years of NED (no evidence of disease/metastasis)! The results mean continued annual care with my ocular oncologist and with an oncologist that includes blood work, CTs of my chest, and MRIs of my liver and abdomen.

More important than ongoing medical care is the way God opened my eyes to the truth of His Word. I have cycled through the grief stages on this journey more than once: anger, isolation and loneliness, denial, and sadness. But I know God causes everything to work together for my good, and I am called according to His purpose (Romans 8:28). When I trust Him, He directs my paths (Proverbs 3:5–6). He tells me to *fear not* 365 times in His Word, one for every day of the year. When I am anxious, I tell God what is on my heart, and He gives me peace that surpasses *all* understanding (Philippians 4:6–7). He gives me fullness of joy (Psalm 16:11) even when I don't feel happy. When I seek Him, I find Him (Jeremiah 29:13). He gives me a future and a hope (Jeremiah 29:11). This is just a snapshot of the verses that have ministered to me through this journey.

For the longest time, I wondered if only six in a million people are diagnosed with ocular melanoma every year, then why me? God never promised me an easy road, but this explanation was just not enough. One day, it finally hit me: I would *not* have the intimate walk with the Lord I have now had I not received this diagnosis. I treasure the intimacy I now have with my Creator.

This is what I want for you, my friend, to know Him intimately, love Him, and seek Him. Open your heart for Him to pursue you. By opening my whole heart to Him, I have learned I never want to stop pursuing Him. I can't tell you how many times in the last six years I have told Him, "I just want all of You, everything You have to give me, Lord."

Adjusting to life after the diagnosis has meant trusting and thanking the Lord every day for complete healing in my body. It has meant talking to the Lord when my eye had breathtakingly sharp pains, double vision, a cataract, and when dealing with other vision and inflammation difficulties that have surfaced. It has meant I could never live my life the same again, that serving Him just on Sunday was not enough. It has meant I could have the relationship with Jesus that He desires with me and I desire with Him. It has meant recognizing that God is not done with me yet, and being Shelby's mom is the greatest gift for which I could ever have dreamed. It has meant understanding God has blessed me with a wonderful husband and family. It has meant walking alongside women in their darkest moments and tenderly sharing God's peace and hope.

Learning to fully rely on God with my whole heart and mind has not been easy. My mind quickly tends to default to the negative, both personally and in the world news. We can plan in every area of our life, but God's purpose will prevail (Proverbs 19:21). He patiently waits for us to submit our will to Him and trust Him. I don't know what the future holds, but I know *who* holds my future. A verse I memorized in college and meditate on to this day is Proverbs 3:5–6 (NKJV): "Trust in the Lord with all your heart, and lean not on your own understanding; In all your ways acknowledge Him, and He shall direct your paths."

In addition to digging into the Word, I sought godly counsel throughout this cancer journey through mentors and books to help work through the grief. I read a book that highlighted the healing of the blind man in John chapter 9. In the first five verses, Jesus answers His disciples' question about why the man was born blind. The disciples wondered if the man was born blind because of his own sins or his parents' sins. I immediately connected with the disciples' proposed reason for the man's blindness, as I had blamed myself when I was first diagnosed. Jesus answered the disciples in verse 3 (NLT): "This happened so the power of God could be seen in him." My heart nearly exploded with love for my Heavenly Father when I read this verse. How marvelous that the God of the universe would use me so His power could be seen and known!

Sweet friend, we will not go anywhere until God says it's time, no matter the battle we face. Isaiah 54:17 tells us that no weapon formed against us will prosper. Do you believe that with all your heart? I have prayed this verse for so many years it is ingrained in me. I really don't think I fully believed this verse with my whole heart until I started walking through this cancer journey with my Savior, my Healer, my Redeemer. Knowing He is in control, you, too, can confidently walk with Him and pray His Word over your life.

Looking at me now, you would never know my body has battled this rare eye cancer. You would also never know how God has worked in my life. We never know what anyone is dealing with at any point in life and what battle anyone faces on any given day. We all have a story. Some of us have more stories than we would like to count. I am just a vessel to share God's goodness and His saving grace. We can trust Him no matter our circumstances.

The greatest lesson learned on this precious walk with Jesus all these years has been to recognize that *now* is the time to pursue my calling to speak life, love, purpose, and hope into the hearts of women. It is *your* time to pursue your God-given calling, too! Think about what God is nudging you to do. Pray about the actions He is calling you to take. Ask God, "What is one thing I can do today to walk in my calling?" It may be as simple as praying for someone or encouraging someone around you with a smile or a few heartfelt words. It could be that you write the testimony God has placed on your heart to share with the world. Nothing is impossible with Him! Just remember, pursue Him every day with your whole heart, not just when tragedy strikes and your world comes crashing down. You will experience the peace, joy, and love that no one or nothing on this earth can give you but Him.

About the Author

SUZANNE STINES HAS BEEN a professional school counselor in North Carolina and Virginia for many years. One of her greatest joys is helping students explore and pursue their college and career dreams. In 2015, the Lord showed her in a vision that she would become an inspirational speaker. In 2016, she became a certified John C. Maxwell speaker, coach, and trainer.

When Suzanne was diagnosed with a rare eye cancer in 2018, her world came crashing down. She felt completely overwhelmed and struggled through every stage of grief. She learned how to chase Jesus and has since pursued a deeper and more intimate walk with God. She will encourage you, make you laugh, and bring you to tears with stories of how God has moved in her life before and after the diagnosis.

Suzanne resides in Richmond, VA with her husband, Logan, and daughter, Shelby. She's had the honor of loving two dogs and plans to have another furry best friend when her life slows down a little. She also loves all things health and wellness and has regularly exercised for nearly three decades. Suzanne speaks, teaches, and ministers to women through various platforms.

You can learn more and connect with Suzanne at suzannestines.com

CHAPTER 26

Overcoming the Fear of Obedience

IT WAS GONE. JUST completely gone. I lost my joy. I was in the darkest place I had been in over twenty-five years. I love the Lord, and I love serving Him, yet I felt so far from Him. My relationship with my Heavenly Father became more and more distant over time. I put on a good face, showed up at church, taught women's classes, led a women's discipleship group, and I was in year sixteen as a public school teacher. Oh, and I'm the preacher's wife.

I thought I had a great plan: I would retire from teaching in five years, enjoy working on our hobby farm, and travel to see our children and grandchildren across the country. I only had five years to go! I was so close, yet I was so miserable. During the Covid pandemic, I saw the need in our school district for more full-time virtual teachers, and I took the leap. I taught virtual school part-time for many years and believed the change would be pretty smooth for me. I was so excited about working from home. Well, I was mistaken. And we know what God says about our plans. "A man's heart plans his way, but the Lord directs his steps" (Proverbs 16:9, NKJV).

Truly, I felt like a Jonah in the unfathomable, dark, miserable pit of the big fish; only my tenure there was three years. Day by day, I sank farther into misery. And the reality of the situation is that I put myself there. I knew it was all on me. After my second year of full-time teaching, God spoke to my heart and told me He had a different plan for my life, but I disregarded the Holy Spirit's direction and disobeyed my Heavenly Father. I continued in my teaching career. I had my own plans, followed my own path for over fourteen years, and ended up in a place I didn't want to be.

Was virtual teaching so terrible? Why did so many of my colleagues seem to love it and thrive while I grew in resentment and frustration daily? Why was I so miserable?

In a word, I was where I was because of disobedience. I was too afraid to say yes to God and pursue the ministry He called me to—speaking and writing. For years, I put off and found any excuse possible not to sit down and write my story, which is a beautiful story of God's intervention in the life of a frightened little girl. Yet, here I am, much older, sixteen years into a career in the public school system, only a few years away from retirement eligibility, and still living in fear. This time, it is fear of obedience.

Why would God want me to write my story, a story I have tried to keep hidden for so many years? Why would God want me to launch into public speaking for women's ministries? He knows everything, yet I continuously reminded Him of all the reasons why I wasn't the right one for this job.

- I'm too old to start a new career.

- I am only five years away from retiring.

- I'm not pretty enough.

- No one wants to listen to me talk.

- I'm not smart enough.

- There are already plenty of books on the market about that.

- I can never be as good as so and so.

I'm not young enough. Oh, I said that one already, didn't I? I tried that with God too. I repeated myself over and over, year after year, explaining again and again why I couldn't do it and why I was not the right woman for this job.

Yet, all the time, my heart wanted to pursue His calling. And rather than embracing this desire, I used it as just another excuse. I kept telling myself and God that the speaking ministry was something I wanted to do; therefore, it wasn't God calling me, but just my selfish desires. I once shared this excuse with a younger, sweet Christian friend, and boldly, she confronted me with the comment, "Susie, have you ever thought that maybe you have that desire in your heart because God put it there?" Humph, that's a really good question.

So, as time kept on drifting, fourteen years after the initial call, my heels still dug in. I was trying to plow my way through my own plans and disobeying God's will for my life.

God is so good, and I am thankful He is so patient with me. He never passed me by, saying, "Fine, I'll just find someone else to do this." Instead, He continues to speak to me through Scripture, songs, sermons, and people.

I began leading a small group of women at my church in a discipleship group (D-group). We started our fifteen-month journey armed with our Bible, a daily reading plan, an empty journal, memorization verses, and a copy of Robby Gallaty's *Growing Up*.[1] Almost every Sunday night, we met to share about our week with Christ and hold each other accountable for following through with the spiritual disciplines of a believer.

Now, I do know a little bit about God's holy Word, as I have a bachelor's degree in biblical studies and have read the Bible from cover to cover multiple times. However, the added task of journaling each time I read helped me not just read a

---

1. Robby Gallaty, *Growing Up: How to Be a Disciple Who Makes Disciples* (B&H Books, 2022).

chapter but take the time to search each chapter to hear what God was saying to me.

Truly, during this time of daily reading, almost everything I read challenged me regarding my disobedience to God's call. Finally, my breaking point came upon reading the story in Acts 19 about the conversion of the magicians. "And many who had believed came confessing and telling their deeds. Also, many of those who had practiced magic brought their books together and burned them in the sight of all. And they counted up the value of them, and it totaled fifty thousand pieces of silver. So the word of the Lord grew mightily and prevailed" (Acts 19:18–20, NKJV).

What? People steeped in magic, upon coming to know Jesus Christ as their Lord and Savior, immediately burned the books by which they made a living! Fifty thousand pieces of silver were equivalent to fifty thousand days' wages at that time, and they just burned it right up.

No one told them to burn those books. But these people were so changed by their brand-new relationship with Jesus that they could not keep doing what they had been doing. They knew they must change the course of their lives, and burning the books was a demonstration that they would not go back to the old way of living. They trusted God would provide for them.

This story slapped me right in the face. I have been a Christian for over forty years, yet I have not "burned the books." I was still holding onto the way I thought I should earn a living rather than trusting God to provide. How could we make it financially if I quit my teaching job? How would we pay our bills? What about retirement? And remember, I am not young enough, pretty enough, smart enough. It just didn't make sense for me to quit.

And where was my husband in all of this? I so wanted him to just tell me what to do. Then, it would all be on his shoulders. But instead of telling me to stay or quit, he spoke these wise words: "God always requires a step of faith before He moves into action."

All these years, God has been trying to tell me, "Behold, I will do a new thing. Now it shall spring forth; shall you not know it? I will even make a road in the wilderness and rivers in the desert" (Isaiah 43:19, NKJV). God was just waiting for me to take that step of faith and truly trust Him with His will for my life. All my excuses fell flat in the face of the radical change in the people of Acts 19. I have finally given all my excuses up to God and surrendered my will to His. Through the daily, consistent reading of God's Word, prayer, and wise, godly counsel, I found truth, conviction, and courage to obey His call.

Not wanting to just walk out on my principal and students, I finished the school year but did not return to teaching the following year.

So, you might wonder how life's going since I took that first step of faith. I have been a "hobby baker" for many years, making and decorating cakes and cupcakes for friends and family, selling a few here and there. God has used my hobby to fill in the financial gap created by my quitting full-time teaching. Two days after telling my D-group friends about my commitment to let go, surrender my plans to Him, and follow God's calling, He went to work. One of my daughter's best friends is the owner of a smallish-town coffee shop, and her supplier of cake pops and biscuits also quit her job, leaving this business owner in need of a new supplier. Guess who makes her cake pops and biscuits now?! In addition to this coffee shop, a virtual co-teacher also opened a new coffee shop and hired me to supply all of her baked goods. Doesn't God have a sense of humor? He has filled in our financial gap using cake pops. I have to laugh about this ironic turn in my life.

Now, I am able to use this God-given talent on a part-time basis to provide baked goods for a few coffee shops in my hometown. My profit would be significantly higher if I could keep all my grands out of the cake pops and my adult son out of my monster cookies.

My other "part-time" hours are spent walking in obedience as I am honing my speaking and writing skills, studying for messages, and writing my story, which is scheduled to be in print soon.

While God has certainly filled the financial gap, there is a greater need He has provided for. By finally surrendering and obeying God, I have written my story. It is a hard story, but it is also a beautiful story because God is the Hero. God has set me free and healed my broken heart created by an abusive childhood. He has removed the bondage of fear, shame, and guilt I have been stumbling around in for many years. Now, I am able to run this race of life, free from the trappings of the past, not looking back to flounder in pain and pity but remembering the wondrous work of my God. He picked me up out of the mire and set my feet on solid ground. And that's not all! I have made the great trade. I traded in my ashes, mourning, and heavy spirit, and now I wear the victor's crown. I have the joy of the Lord and garments of praise (Isaiah 61:1–3).

My faith has been tested, and although it took me a long time to overcome my fear of obedience, God is faithful and is using my story of healing and freedom to help other women run their best race of life. As I focus on the healing God has given me, I am able to share with women through retreats, Bible studies, and my writing adventures how they, too, can find this healing. I often hear from women who attended retreats where I was the guest speaker, and they thrill my heart and soul as they share how they are experiencing joy and freedom.

I regret that it took me so many years to surrender and overcome the fear of obedience, but I am thankful God is patient and loving, and especially that He never gives up on us. I must now fix my eyes forward, letting go of the regrets and what-ifs of years of opportunities missed. I cannot waste more time wallowing in the "if only" but dwell on the One and Only—the One who truly satisfies and provides exactly what we need.

Are you stalling out in your life because you suffer from the fear of obedience? Is there something you've been putting off, afraid of stopping or starting? Does the task God has called you to put you out of your comfort zone? I encourage you to take your first step of faith, then watch and see how God moves into action.

Be faithful to daily Bible intake, as this is often how God speaks to us. If you are not already practicing a daily reading and journaling plan, consider starting one today. I highly recommend Robby Gallaty's H.E.A.R. model, as found in

Growing Up.[2] Listen for and follow God's promptings. He's never wrong. His plan is the best plan. While it may not be easy, God promises to lead and guide us and never leave us. After all, it's His plan, His new thing, and He makes all things work together for our good and His glory (Romans 8:28).

2. Robby Gallaty, *Growing Up: How to Be a Disciple Who Makes Disciples* (B&H Books, 2022).

About the Author

As a Christian speaker and author, **Susie Lewis** loves to encourage and equip women to go from wandering in life to wondering in God. Whether sharing with women at a weekend retreat, leading a Bible study, or sipping an oat milk latte in the coffee shop, she motivates women to live a life of joy and freedom that is found by breaking free from the bondage of the past.

Susie loves to teach, and she loves to laugh. Utilizing her ever-growing understanding of God's Word, she teaches with passion and integrity and shares a lot of laughter and smiles all the while.

Susie's messages are always Christ centered and based on foundational truths in the Bible. Working and playing on the family farm provides Susie with plenty of fun and inspirational insights, which she weaves into her speaking and writing. She helps her audience see God at work in everyday things and in everyday ways.

Although growing in her biblical knowledge while earning her degree in biblical studies, Susie has found the real key to spiritual transformation—the discipline of daily intake of God's Word. She has experienced firsthand the life-changing power of reading, journaling, applying, and praying through God's Word. Her heart desires to empower women to join her on this beautiful journey of life.

Bless the Lord, O my soul,
And forget not all His benefits:
Who forgives all your iniquities,
Who heals all your diseases,
Who redeems your life from destruction,
Who crowns you with lovingkindness and tender mercies.
Psalm 103:2–4 (NKJV)

Who doesn't want a crown of lovingkindness and tender mercies? Susie has hers, and she loves to share with women how to get theirs.

Connect with Susie via email: susielewisspeaker@gmail.com

Website: susielewis.net

CHAPTER 27

He Knows You by Name

"AND WHO ARE YOU again?"

Even though it was the fifth time he had asked me that question in just a few hours, I smiled and answered, "I am your youngest daughter, Tracey, Dad."

I grew up on a ranch in Southeast Arizona, and my dad was someone I knew to be a tough, hardworking, honest, and devoted husband and father. He was fearless. He dropped out of high school a month before graduation to enlist in the Army and fight in the Korean War. As a sharpshooter, he fought on the front lines for sixteen months. He said he thought the battalion command had forgotten him there. When asked how he went from a private to sergeant first class in such a short time, he replied, "It was the process of elimination." Dad saw a lot of death and destruction, but he was still a kind and loving man. He didn't often tell us he loved us, but he showed it.

When I was six, we moved to a large ranch an hour south of the farm. The ranch was around 30,000 acres—big enough to run several hundred head of cattle.

Farming drastically differs from ranching, but Dad was equipped to handle both professions. My mom always called him "a jack of all trades and a master of one." He was a master electrician but was able to do anything. He remodeled the old ranch house, ran equipment, welded, doctored animals, and did any other job needed. He was the strongest and most incredible man I knew.

As a farmer who later turned rancher, it wasn't ideal for Dad to have five girls and no boys. There was no son to help carry the workload, but when it mattered most, five daughters stepped up to help carry him.

Have you ever experienced an impact event? You know, when life is going along routinely, and then the impact happens—when one catastrophic event changes your life forever and leaves you wondering how you'll make it through. Our family's impact event happened when we lost our mom in 2011. It changed us forever, and it brought the strong man we knew as Dad to his knees.

My mom went into the emergency room with a stomachache, and a short nine days later, we all stood at her bedside as she passed away. It rocked our world and devastated our dad. The impact event was the beginning of the end for Dad.

I remember gathering in a group the night she passed. Dad wasn't in the hospice room. He couldn't stand to see the woman he was married to for over sixty years leave his side. And when we met to tell him she was gone, a light went out in his soul. It was a light that would never come on again.

The weeks after the fateful night were hard. We each took time to stay with him. We attempted to help him learn to function without her, but he slowly slipped further and further into despair. Once the reality of her never returning hit him, he just seemed to give up. The strong man I knew as a child and young adult started to vanish before my eyes.

During this time, I reminded my dad of God's blessings. We experienced a devastating blow, but God showered His blessings on our family. Mom and Dad were blessed with a long marriage, five daughters, sixteen grandkids, and over thirty great grandkids to show for it. We were all blessed.

Seeing God's goodness in difficult times can be challenging, but we should stop amidst the chaos and remember how good and kind He is to us. Life's trials are never easy or fun, but they strengthen us. God has a plan, and He works all things for the good of those who love Him (Romans 8:28). Dad never openly proclaimed a love for God, but he could see the blessings when we pointed them out.

The upset of our lives continued, and it took some convincing, but we eventually persuaded our dad to move in next to my oldest sister. Things hit a new rhythm for a short time, but Dad remained on a slow and steady decline. Every day, he remembered less and relied upon others' assistance more.

He started having panic attacks. When the sun set, he often showed up at my sister's door in a full-blown panic. Then came the fateful day they were out feeding animals, and Dad's leg snapped. The femur in his leg literally broke in two, and he was rushed to the hospital. We went back to taking shifts during the day, and due to the anesthesia from surgery, Dad's mental health took a drastic turn for the worse. He often didn't know where he was, and the panic attacks increased in frequency and intensity.

As the effects of the anesthesia gradually wore off, there was a slight improvement, but our dad remained a shell of a man. He continued to decline mentally and physically, and there was nothing we could do but sit and watch.

They moved him to a rehab facility for physical therapy. However, he continued to complain of pain, and when my sister insisted they take another X-ray, they found the hardware placed in his leg in surgery was protruding into his muscle. It meant another surgery and recovery. We had to start all over.

Two surgeries and months and months of therapy left us with a dad who forgot to eat and sat in isolation if one of us girls was not with him. When we were there, he often sat in silence. I found it difficult to engage him in conversation because he didn't seem to remember anything.

His dementia gradually progressed into Alzheimer's. As time passed, we all began to slip from his memory. He pointed to a picture on the wall and said, "Now I know that's me, but who is that woman and the girls with me?" Dad didn't know any of us.

One of the last times I went to spend time with him, he looked at me and asked, "Are you the therapist?"

"No, Dad," I said, "I am your youngest daughter, Tracey." We went for a drive that day, and every twenty minutes or so, he looked over at me and asked the same question, to which I smiled and reminded him I was his daughter.

Watching someone we love slowly slip away is never easy, but God never forsakes us. We saw God work in every situation as we entered the Covid crisis. We had found a lady willing to spend time with Dad a few months prior. She gave him companionship, even if it was just sitting with him in silence. When she approached us about moving him into her home for full-time care, we all agreed that would be good for him. We moved him just days before the home he was in locked down tight, and if Dad had still been there, we would have had no access to him.

God was gracious, and He worked everything for our good. Dad only lived a short time longer, and God made sure his girls were with him. It was a bittersweet time, but it made me realize how close we all drew to our dad in the final years and days of his life. It wasn't easy to take time out of our busy lives and sit with someone who didn't know us, but it was always rewarding. I learned to tell my dad that I loved him, which is a word that never flowed freely from our lips while we were growing up. Every time I saw him, I made it a point to say, "I love you, Dad." I can still hear his voice saying, "I love you too," which is worth everything.

People may forget our names, but God doesn't. God has called us out of the darkness and into the light. He is your kind, loving Father who always knows your name. When we care for another, we demonstrate God's love and kindness. Those nine years were tough, but they allowed each of us to take time out of our busy lives and draw closer to the amazing man we called Dad.

Whether we take time to care for our loved ones or spend time with God, we give up time we could spend doing other things. However, time spent doing both adds immeasurable benefits to our lives. I wouldn't trade time doing either for time spent doing something less valuable. Ultimately, God is the cornerstone of our lives, and our families nurture and love us here on earth. Never feel guilty when you serve the Lord or your family. We are called to a life of service, and we'll never get back the time we wish we would have spent doing the truly important things.

About the Author

Tracey Glenn is a writer, speaker, and entrepreneur. She writes and teaches from the lessons she learned in church, life, and growing up on a cattle ranch.

Tracey has authored the following books:

Gathering the Wayward Heart, Lessons on Faith, Trust, and Surrendering Our Best-Laid Plans
Seeking Peace in Every Season, 12-Week Devotional and Journal
Seeking Love in Every Season, 12-Week Devotional and Journal
Seeking Joy in Every Season, 12-Week Devotional and Journal

Tracey is happily married to her husband of thirty-five years, Link, and is a mother of three and grandmother of four. She is a special needs mom, adoptive mom, homeschool mom, caregiver, and business owner, and she gives God the glory for everything.

Connect with Tracey at:
Website: traceyglenn.com
Facebook: Tracey Glenn Author-Speaker
Instagram: @brandedinfaith

CHAPTER 28

I Surrender All

TODAY IS MY FORTY-FOURTH birthday, and it's not exactly like I'd envisioned it. Birthdays are supposed to be happy, joyous occasions, but instead, it's me sitting alone again at another event for one of my children. My heart aches as I listen to moms talking about plans for their families, complaining about the socks their husbands left next to the laundry basket or the trash he forgot to take out. I am going home to an empty bed, missing the sound of my husband's beautiful voice singing "Happy Birthday," something I only get to hear if I play a video.

One beautiful January afternoon, my world changed in a way I never dreamed it would. The day was almost too perfect. The sun was shining instead of the usual January rain, and our children were playing outside. My sweet four-month-old lay sleeping on the bed between my husband and me as we were planning our second trip to Gatlinburg. And then came the words, "I don't feel good," followed by "I need you to call an ambulance." Fifteen minutes later, Brian was in the arms of Jesus while my hands were doing CPR. My amazing, selfless, faithful husband was only forty years old when a massive heart attack ended his life.

Brian had so much to live for! His dream of opening his own store was finally coming to fruition. Just the week before he passed, we took a trip to begin the process of buying into a franchise, something we started planning and saving for a decade prior. I wasn't sure how it would work out, but each time I questioned him, Brian replied, "Trust the process." I remember the last night we were in Galveston, standing on the back deck, overlooking the bay as the sun set. Brian was happy and had a peace about him that I don't know if I'd ever seen before, outside of our wedding day. His dream was so close; our plan of bringing him home from the brutal hours he worked was just a few years away. But in the blink of an eye, he was gone, his dream was gone, and I was a widow.

As I stood over his body on our bed, I begged God to leave him with me. I *needed* him. I didn't know how to live without him, how to survive, how to breathe. And I didn't want to. He was my rock, my everything. But in those moments, as Brian was taking his last breath, I felt the amazing presence of God like never before. He whispered almost audibly, *Trust Me.*

Brian was the breadwinner, I was the stay-at-home mom, and I was scared to continue or even look to the future. So many thoughts plowed through my head at once. "How will I feed my five children and keep my home?" "Why God?" Even as my heart was breaking, Brian went from my hands to the hands of Jesus while God filled me with such incredible, amazing peace. I knew beyond a shadow of a doubt God had us.

A portrait of us from November 2021 hangs on my bedroom wall facing my bed. The two of us, standing side by side, laughing at the camera—me holding on to his shirt as if I knew what would come. It is the first thing I see every morning when I wake up. We were full of laughter and smiles the afternoon we took the picture, not knowing what was to come. I was proud of that picture, proud of the years of support I'd given him, proud of the eighteen years of marriage we were about to celebrate, proud to be his wife.

Someone took this beautiful photo and cropped Brian's handsome face for his obituary—the announcement of his death. The photo was posted all over social media; to this day, if you google my name, his picture is the first thing you see.

Seeing it, I realized I was no longer part of a pair, a half to a whole, a wife to my husband. The woman I was the morning of January 29, 2021, suddenly ceased to be. I was a widow.

In the days that followed, I was in a fog, overwhelmed with the mountain of tasks before me. My priority was telling my sweet babies—ages fourteen, thirteen, nine, four, and four months—that their hero was gone. It was my responsibility to help them begin the process of grieving, knowing their hearts would never be whole again. I had so many decisions to make, starting with where to bury my best friend, and I had a service to plan. People asked me questions I couldn't answer, such as, "Was I going to continue to stay at home? Was I going to put the children in public school? How would I support them? Would I sell my home?" Each question piled on top of the one before it.

And then the comments came, as if my husband being gone somehow permitted them to say whatever intrusive thought popped into their head. Someone callously pointed out my four-year-old would barely remember his daddy, and my sweet baby girl never would. Did they think I hadn't thought of this? Between trauma and grief, my breastmilk suddenly stopped producing, which added to my heartache even more. Over and over, I cried out to God, and I felt Him say, "My daughter, trust Me." But I didn't know how. I couldn't see a way forward. I was so very lost without my Brian.

I had absolutely no idea who I was on my own. I thrived on planning, making lists, and being in complete control of life and my emotions. My children rarely saw me cry. I had it all handled. But suddenly, I did not. I felt like I was drowning, trying my best to grab onto a rope, but the rope kept slipping through my fingers. I remember crying to my best friend about how I wanted to stay exactly the woman I was in our beautiful last picture, exactly how he remembered me. She pointed out that I wasn't the same girl I was when he married me. The highs and lows of our lives changed who we both were. In her straightforward, loving way, she told me either I could fight it or embrace it. Change has never been something I've handled with grace, and even worse when I have no control. But giving up control meant giving it all to God. I was angry at Him, yet begging to see the good in this. To see that Brian's death meant something. Sitting in church one Sunday morning, I heard this song.

It is well, with my soul
It is well, it is well,
With my soul.

It is well with my soul. Hearing those words, I froze with tears running down my face. At that moment, I certainly couldn't say that about myself, not even in my relationship with God. The peace I felt when Brian died was gone. I couldn't feel God, I couldn't see Him, and no amount of crying out made me feel like He was with me. All the Bible teachings from the decades before told me God was there, but emotionally, I didn't know where He was. I was angry, I was lost, I was lonely, and I was hurting. My goal was to meet all my children's needs and ensure they were healing.

Our schedules resumed as normal—dance, church, track, and homeschool. Being both mom and dad at the same time didn't leave me any time to grieve. Even over a year after Brian's death, I truly had not begun to process this immense loss. I didn't know what to do with the anger, crushing pain, and yearning for my husband. As is normal with life-changing events, our friends who were supportive of me when Brian first died went back to their lives. Those who had memories of him that I desperately wanted to hear returned to work, and time stopped for no one except me. My struggles were hidden because I was so busy, except for my dearest friend, who lived almost three hours away. To ease this pain, at least temporarily, I made decisions that I would never have dreamed of doing. Then, as God often allows to get our attention, I hit rock bottom. Hard.

Realizing how lost I was, I finally reached out to a therapist who was an absolute gift from God. Without her, I probably wouldn't be writing this. She made me realize that while I brushed off the label of trauma, I was dealing with the stress of trauma. I needed to allow myself the space to understand I was hurt and injured, and no amount of internal strength could fix it. I had to let go. So often, our sessions ended in sobbing and prayers. I gave myself permission to explore my deepest, darkest hurts and confront my anger and fears. I began to trust God again.

Numerous blessings have come from Brian's death. I know it sounds odd after such a tragic loss, but it's true. After meeting with the funeral director, I went back to my house filled with people. My friend came in with a cooler of donated breast milk from hours away. Another cooler was found on my seat after the funeral—just one of many miracles, showing me God was watching over me. Another blessing is the incredible bond my children and I have that we would not have otherwise.

Jeremiah 29:12 (NIV) says, "You will seek me and find me when you seek me with all your heart."

I have been a Christian for over thirty years, but now I have a completely different relationship with the Lord. It's one where I question, and He answers, even when it is not what I want to hear. My faith in His plan for my life is more than I ever imagined it could be, which only happened because I was at the lowest point I possibly could be. And still, He was there, loving me.

Now, here we are, almost three years later. My babies all look like me, but each one is a little of Brian's personality. Oh, how I wish he could see how amazing they are! There's so much I want to tell him. The desire of my heart is to let my husband's legacy live on, and it truly does.

My oldest plays guitar, just like Brian did, and one day, I pray that a very special girl will fall in love with him just like I did with his daddy. My oldest daughter has her father's dry, sharp sense of humor. She knows just the thing to say when my heart is heavy. My sweet middle child was Daddy's girl. She loves people like Jesus does, just like Brian did. She's never met a stranger and is always quick to serve others. My spunky little guy still asks for Daddy hugs. He is so smart and loves big words—something that doesn't come from me. And my precious baby girl, who only knew her daddy for four months, is full of his fire for life.

And me. I embraced the changes, although somewhat reluctantly at times, not just from trauma but from God working in my life. Looking at Julie in the picture from November 2021, the wife of Brian, half of a whole, and looking at Julie in the summer of 2024, Brian's widow, single mom, I'm not the same person. Looking at the precious picture of the two of us, I don't even recognize the girl staring back at me.

The changes started little by little, and all seemed to be utterly out of my control. The color red, my signature color, the color of my wedding shoes, the color of my first couch, and the color of my dress in our picture is no longer my favorite color. Instead, it was replaced with pink—bright Barbie pink, soft pink, and all the shades in between. I changed my hair from brunette to the blonde Brian met nineteen years before. But those were just on the surface. Other changes went much deeper. My desire to be utterly and completely in control was gone. The incessant need to plan no longer existed. Oh, how Brian used to mock my colored pens and notebooks full of lists. But I couldn't even make one to order groceries. I learned very quickly that nothing was in my control except trusting God.

In moments of grief and trauma, just thinking ahead from day to day was beyond difficult. I didn't have the time or the emotional energy to keep up with those lists. More important than the list making was falling in love with my children again. Of course, I'd always loved them, but that need for control, that worrying about what others saw or how they might or might not behave, kept me from doing fun things like putting on my swimsuit or walking in and out of shops or just laying on my bed with them hours past their bedtime. I found freedom not just in letting go of who I was but also in who I was becoming. I no longer worried about what people thought about my decisions or how I grieved. God has truly shaped and molded me into a woman I could have never been. I love her far more than I did the girl looking back at me from my prized portrait. And I think Brian would as well.

Shortly after Brian's death, my pastor approached me about writing a book. I laughed. I am a homeschooling mama, a solo parent to five children, and I thought, "When will I write a book?" I promised him I'd pray about it. At the same time, God started speaking to my heart. "Tell your story." Surely, not many people could relate or even want to hear the sad story about the death of my husband, and I certainly did not want pity. But he planted a seed, and now you are reading some of its fruit.

Do you see yourself in my story? Maybe not in the death of your husband or wife, but perhaps in the loss of a marriage or job or something happened in your life that left you feeling out of control. Utter and complete loss, wondering where God was taking you and why He allowed the situation to happen. Have you sat there and just cried out to God, begging Him to fix the situation, reverse time, and restore your life to the moment before it seemingly went off the rails? I understand because I've been there.

Have you stopped trying to control what you can't and just dropped it all in front of God? Brian's favorite quote was, "Trust the process," which, to him, meant, "Trust in God, and follow His plan," even when we can't see it. At times, I was frustrated when he said this because trusting the process meant giving complete control to God. Not trusting God completely meant I thought I knew better than He did. But I don't. I can't see where God is taking me or what He has planned for tomorrow, let alone the next chapter of my life. But what I do know is that no matter what happens with my life, God has already planned out the future. I can truly say, "It is well with my soul."

My words of wisdom to you are the same words Brian told me countless times, "Trust the process." Proverbs 3:5–6 (NIV) says, "Trust in the Lord with all your heart and lean not on your own understanding; in all your ways submit to him, and he will make your paths straight." As you trust in Him, He will do more than you can ever hope or imagine.

About the Author

MEET **JULIE NAPP**. FROM the outside looking in, she appeared to have a perfect life: homeschool mom to five children, an amazing husband, vibrant role at church, and critical connections with her community. And then one day, without warning, God suddenly called her loving husband home, leaving her a widow at the age of forty-one.

While searching for God's plan for her future, Julie realized He was calling her to become a speaker and an author, something she had dreamed of as a young girl. Julie speaks to the woman trying to find God's plan for her life amidst all the chaos in the world.

She calls the Mississippi Gulf Coast home, where she enjoys baking, reading Christian fiction, and saving "eventual" projects to her Pinterest boards.

You can connect with her and follow her work at JulieNapp.com

CHAPTER 29

Courage After Loss

SAYING YES AGAIN

MY HAND TREMBLED AS I gripped the test. When two bright blue lines popped up in the window, I burst into tears.

"No, God!" I cried. "How can I do this again? I can't lose another one."

"Lord, let it stick." I prayed. "Hold this little one tight."

Over that past year, three of my babies silently slipped from my womb right into Jesus's arms. And my grieving mama heart didn't think it could bear the deep cut of pain again. Despite my desperate longing for another baby, the possibility of losing this new life filled me with panic.

I wanted more children, but surrendering the unknown and placing all control in God's hands was grueling. Yet, I knew what He was asking me to do. *Even if* my heart was shattered again, God wanted me to be brave.

"God, give me strength," I whispered. "Give me strength . . ."

And for the next nine months, this simple prayer became my lifeline.

It was my prayer when I started bleeding, and I thought I'd lost her.

It was my prayer when my all-day morning sickness kept my head in the toilet and me away from being the hands-on mama my three-year-old daughter needed.

It was my prayer when my mind played around with all the what-if scenarios and fed my deepest fears.

And it was my prayer when one last push delivered a healthy baby girl into my arms.

Truthfully, in those moments of uncertainty, the weary whispers of "God give me strength" didn't feel very courageous. But does true courage really feel like courage when we're walking through life's storms, trying to be brave?

Or—can courage be something more subtle? Maybe it's one day looking back when all the dust settles and realizing you did face your greatest fears, even though you felt like you had no idea what you were doing and were oh, so weak. Despite the unknown, you still chose to keep putting one foot in front of the other.

Recently, I came across a quote by the French American author Anais Nin. She said, "Life shrinks or expands in proportion to one's courage."

As I sat with this idea, I reflected on my own life and how one simple "yes" after another—to try something new or to try something again that had once failed before—led me step-by-step down the road of my life's story, of God's story asking me to trust Him. Many of the good gifts in my life were simply the result of trusting God and resolving to do the hard things He asked of me, even when I wanted to run away and hide.

Whenever I feel timid and weak, I often think about the Old Testament prophet Elijah. He's such a relatable guy because, in one minute, he's bold and confident, confronting King Ahab and the Baal priests. And the next minute, he's running for his life, hiding in a cave.

In 1 Kings 16:30, we read that King Ahab "did evil in the sight of the Lord." In fact, Scripture tells us that Ahab had done more to provoke God than all the kings of Israel who lived before him. (When you read about how awful the other kings of the Bible were, Ahab must have done *a lot* of provoking!) To add to his less-than-desirable persona, Ahab married the deplorable Queen Jezebel. Together, they chose to serve and worship the pagan god Baal instead of the one true God of Israel. This dysfunctional dynamic set the stage for the deep corruption Elijah faced.

As the Lord's prophet, Elijah wanted God to demonstrate His power in front of Israel and bring the false god Baal and his followers to ruin. So, Elijah proposed a challenge to the people of Israel and Ahab's Baal priests. He suggested, "Let's set up two altars—one to Baal and the other to the true God of Israel. On each altar, we'll place an ox with some wood. And neither of us will light them. Then, let's pray and see which God sends fire to consume it" (1 Kings 18:22–24, my paraphrase). All the people thought it was a good idea.

So, Elijah and the Baal prophets prepared their altars, but Elijah decided to spice his up. He poured so much water on the wood and the ox that "the water flowed around the altar" (vs. 35).

That evening, Elijah and all of Israel witnessed a miracle. "The fire of the Lord fell and consumed the burnt offering and the wood, and the stones and the dust; and it licked up the water that was in the trench. When all the people saw this, they fell on their faces; and they said, 'The Lord, He is God; the Lord, He is God!'" (1 Kings 18:38–39, NASB).

Can you imagine being there and witnessing God's consuming fire devour every bit of Elijah's sopping-wet sacrifice? Most of us will probably never see anything like this. But Elijah did.

And afterward, he bravely pursued the Baal priests and annihilated them. (Yes, those times were brutal!)

However, right after this miracle, in the next chapter, King Ahab told his wicked wife, Jezebel, about all the things Elijah had done to destroy their Baal god and prophets. In her fury, she threatened to take Elijah's life.

Brave and bold one day. Then, running in fear for his life and hiding in caves soon after. Life is like this sometimes, isn't it? I sure can relate to these two extremes, can't you? Except, unlike Elijah, I don't run and hide in caves when I need to retreat (though sometimes I wish I could). Instead, I hide in my bathroom closet. If my family loses me, they know where to look. There, sitting on the floor, they'll find me, usually eating chocolate.

God and I have worked out a lot of problems on that closet floor, chocolate in hand.

I've often told Him, "I can't keep doing all this anymore. You've asked too much of me." And He quietly reminds me, "My grace is sufficient for you, for my power is made perfect in weakness" (2 Corinthians 12:9, NIV).

Elijah cried out to God, too, and in his weakness, God sent angels to feed him bread and water to give him strength for the task ahead. Instead of chastising Elijah for being exhausted and afraid, God reminded him of His love and mercy. And yet, God still had work for Elijah to do (as He does for us), but He patiently waited until Elijah regained his strength. Elijah eventually stood back up and embarked on the mission God had planned. There was still a king to anoint and a new prophet to appoint.

I think we can all relate to Elijah's story. God doesn't usually ask His children to take the easy road. Sometimes, the journeys ahead take all our strength, with dangers to battle around every treacherous bend. Often, we are afraid to say yes to God because of the certain hardships we know we'll face. But if we continue seeking and listening for His voice, even when hiding in a cave (or bathroom closet), God will meet us where we are and whisper where we should go next.

When we say yes to God, He promises He'll go beside us with every uncertain step, just as He went with Elijah and the way He stayed with my family after losing our babies so many years ago. We know that "the Lord is near to the brokenhearted and saves those who are crushed in spirit" (Psalm 34:18, NASB).

There's no doubt God was there, mourning beside us during our seasons of heartbreak and celebrating in our joy at the births of our precious daughters. I even think God laughed a little when I carried the daughter I so desperately prayed "to stick" past my due date and then begged Him to "please unstick her now."

I would love to say, "And we all lived happily ever after." But honestly, like most of you, our life hasn't exactly played out like a Disney movie. We've had our share of mountaintop moments and deep valleys. I've struggled with years of living in chronic pain, spiritual attacks on our family and business, health concerns with my husband and parents, and one of our precious daughters has a life-threatening condition. Yet, it's in the deepest valleys with God that I've felt Him the nearest. And in those depths, I hear His voice clearest.

As 2 Corinthians 4:8–9 reminds us, "We are hard pressed on every side, but not crushed; perplexed, but not in despair; persecuted, but not abandoned; struck down, but not destroyed."

If today you're feeling weak and fragile, that's okay. I do too. I'm again sitting in an uncertain season of waiting and trusting God to show up. The unknown future lingers ahead, and at times, my mind and body don't feel up to the challenge of this new assignment.

I'm so thankful our God doesn't expect us to always be strong. It's through the painful process of dying to ourselves that Christ magnifies Himself through us. We all know life will get tough at times. But when it does, it's up to us to choose where we lean. When we lean into our Heavenly Father instead of our fleshy fears and lay our weary heads on His shoulders, He grips His gentle arms around us and gives us His strength. It's right there in His loving arms where He transforms our timid spirits into the courageous women He created us to be.

About the Author

MACKI SMITH IS A writer, business owner, and homeschooling mom to three curly-headed daughters. She and her family live on a farm in rural Mississippi with cows, horses, chickens, dogs, cats, and a fish named Charlotte.

Before raising a family, Macki taught kindergarten and special education and led her church's women's ministry. Now, she spends her days helping her husband manage their veterinary practice while schooling her daughters and ministering to women along the way.

She enjoys sharing stories through writing about faith, family, and farm life. As the adage goes, the days are long, and the years are short, so she's making the most of the years of having her little ones at home. On any given day, you may find her with a strong cup of coffee in hand, chasing the kids back into the house, the chickens back into their coop, or the cows back into the pasture.

You can connect with Macki on her website, macki-smith.com, and through her Facebook group, The Peace-Seeking Woman.

CHAPTER 30

The Dream Maker

WITH TEARS STREAMING DOWN my cheeks, I pulled over and prayed, "Okay, Lord, You know best. I can't imagine a better dream, but if this isn't Your plan, I surrender. You must have something even more amazing in store." Still, my heart was breaking as my dream slipped away. I watched a jet streak across the sky, its trail feeling like a final wave goodbye. I was a pilot, but I was sick—and pilots can't fly when they're sick, especially not as sick as I was.

Yet, there was no confirmed diagnosis. In his unmistakable German accent, the gastroenterologist said, "We know something is coming. We don't know what it is yet. It could be MS, or lupus, or some other autoimmune disease, but something is coming." Oh, we did every test possible to discover what was coming and why I was in so much pain, but there were no answers, only more questions.

The list of doctors was extensive, but along the way, there were countless miracles—each one a reminder that hope was never far from reach. The first specialist I saw was an allergist who had interned at a lupus clinic. He was one of the first signs that God was watching over me during this difficult time. He asked a gazillion questions, took more blood than I thought I had to spare, and sent it out for diagnosis. He knew what he was looking for but said nothing about his theory to me. However, for the first time in a long time, I felt heard, and that was enough.

Then there was the gall bladder surgeon who finally said, "Let's wait and see what the allergist finds," after I'd spent an unimaginable night in the ER due to a massive allergic reaction to the pills I took *before* the test he wanted me to take. Needless to say, the test was canceled.

The neurologist said, "You look like an intelligent young woman. I can run the tests your doctor ordered, but they may do more harm than good. My recommendation is to *run*; don't walk out of this hospital." I took his advice and didn't return any time soon.

My symptoms were as extensive as the doctors and tests, like eye-piercing headaches, aches and pains mimicking a marathon I didn't run, and debilitating fatigue. It wasn't the kind of fatigue that makes you wonder if you need to eat better or start taking vitamins. It was the unexplainable-with-words kind of fatigue. When I try to explain, it comes out this way: Imagine you just moved the last box out of a home you've sold and then cleaned for hours so the next homeowner doesn't think you actually lived there. Then you walk out to your overstuffed car with a broom you wish you could throw, rags you will throw, cleaners, and the last roll of toilet paper. You wish you could go home and sleep, but your new home isn't prepared to give you a good night's sleep yet. That's how tired I was—all the time.

There was nothing left to do, and no one left to turn to except the Lord, and I sought Him with every fiber of my being. Of course, He had the perfect healing plan, unconventional and unknown to me, but perfect, nonetheless.

I found a naturopathic doctor, and that's where the healing began. First, there were all the questions and the usual poking and prodding. But I left the doctor's office with a plan and useful tools that included a canister of powder to replace solid food (mix it with water), an at-home enema kit (oh yay!), and an appointment to see him in a week. The one-week fast turned into ninety days. It was a great weight-loss program, but most importantly, it gave my stomach the rest it needed to start on solid food again. The transition to solid food was painstakingly slow. My menu started and ended with steamed zucchini. While we think our bodies cannot be sustained, much less heal, on steamed zucchini, I'm living proof they can.

My family thought I lost my mind choosing alternative healthcare, but I leaned into God, holding fast to His promises like a lifeline in a storm. I understood this was a divinely led healing journey, with every single detail carefully constructed by Almighty God. I only needed to be obedient to Him.

There was little improvement for a year. In fact, I didn't see much improvement until year two, and even then, minor seems too big a word to use to explain the difference. But I celebrated each milestone, no matter how small. I remember feeling an inexplicable joy the day I actually cleaned my entire home—not just one room at a time—only to slink away to bed, hurting and exhausted. I cleaned like a rockstar and still had enough energy to slay the rest of the day. It was a turning point. After two years of fasting, juicing, enemas, reading, visualizing, and praying, I was strong enough to clean my house. Not a big deal to most, but wildly significant to me.

It took three years to heal from lupus. Yes, I finally received the long-awaited diagnosis. In those one thousand plus days, I sat at Jesus' feet every spare moment. I called upon Him often, and He came to me as often as I called. I'd shut my eyes, and He appeared in a somewhat vision-like state, standing above me, surrounded by darkness but with a soft, warm light illuminating His entire being. His robe appeared to sway as if stirred by a gentle breeze. His palms were turned outward, arms open and slightly bent at the elbow, inviting me to receive the healing I so desperately desired. I believe He poured out His healing power upon me, and I humbly received it, one moment at a time.

While this vision may seem a bit out there, the veil lifted ever so slightly to reveal a glimpse into the heavenly realm as I hovered near death's door. Jesus was so close in those difficult days. He remains close, faithful, and ready to help His children.

He is waiting with open arms to give us what we need and to shower us with mercy.

Just as God led me through every step of my healing to wholeness, He planned my next steps too. Jeremiah 29:11 (AMPC) says, "For I know the thoughts *and* plans that I have for you, says the Lord, thoughts *and* plans for welfare *and* peace and not for evil, to give you hope in your final outcome." I hoped in Him, and even though I didn't know what was next, He did. He was already working on more dreams—dreams I didn't know I had, for He is the Dream Maker.

As my body healed, the Lord, in His infinite mercy, gifted me a most beloved title: Mommy. I hadn't imagined that children were a part of my future, nor did I realize how deeply they would fill the longings of my heart, but God knew. When my first son was born, I fell madly in love with him. From the moment I held him, I experienced a love so profound that it changed me forever. God blessed me with three precious little boys in just four years, and my heart nearly bursts with love for each of them. Though I would have welcomed more, time was not on my side. By the age of thirty-nine, I found myself with a three-year-old, a one-year-old, and a newborn. That was it; time had run out, but not before we received our three miracles.

Psalm 37:4 (AMPC) says, "Delight yourself also in the Lord, and He will give you the desires *and* secret petitions of your heart." I delight in the Lord. I praise Him every day, and He has, indeed, given me the desires of my heart many times over. Why? Because they were His desires all along. I've spent a lifetime learning that His ways will always far exceed mine. As I surrender to Him and ask Him to replace my desires with His, He overdoes, overdelivers, and overwhelms me with dream after dream and miracle after miracle.

If you're living in the midst of shattered dreams, remember that God is the ultimate Dream Maker. He has more dreams in store for you than your mind and heart can imagine. Pursuing what I thought was *my* dream didn't work, as my tear-stained cheeks and broken heart so long ago revealed. But God had something far better in store then, and He's not finished yet. I find myself hanging onto the hem of His robe as He moves at a pace that's light years ahead of me. I pray for increased capacity and a willing heart to serve Him in all He has planned before my time here ends.

Jeremiah 29:11 assures us God's plans are the best. I guarantee He has a plan that will take you to newer heights, day after day, year after year, and for the rest of your life. Allow God to walk with you, run ahead of you, pick you up, and fly you sky-high as your dreams take flight. All for His glory. It's all about Him. He is the Great I Am.

About the Author

ANDREA LENDE IS A best-selling author and speaker whose ministry inspires women all over the globe to draw closer to God. She is a prolific writer who loves sharing God's love through devotions, prayers, journals, and Bible reading plans.

Andrea knows the power of reading the Word daily and how it changes hearts and then lives. The podcasts she hosts are a direct reflection of this belief: *Downloads from God* and *Reading the Bible Cover to Cover in 365 Days*. She is a champion for other writers, a book coach, a publisher, and the founder and CEO of Beatitudes Publishing, LLC.

Andrea is a wife and a mother to three adult children. She's called Colorado her home for more than three decades.

Andrea has authored the following books:

Read the Bible Cover to Cover in 365 Days: Discovering God's Heart Through His Word
90 Day Prayer Journal: Drawing Closer to God Through Prayer
It's A Wrap: A Christmas Devotional For Moms
Bible Doodle Journal: Color AND Doodle Your Way Through the Bible
Life After Lupus: What's Your Autoimmune Name?
Meet Jesus in Matthew, Mark, Luke, and John: Devotions, Prayers, and Study Guide for the Gospels
God's Whispers and Melodies: A Heart Transformed Through Music and Lyrics
A Mother's Love: Leaving a Legacy Through Poems and Prayers
God is Still ALMIGHTY! 90 Daily Devotions
Coffee and a Prayer: 90 Peaceful Prayers

You can connect with Andrea by email at andrea@andrealende.com
To connect on Amazon: https://www.amazon.com/author/andrealende
She's most active on Facebook: @andrea.lende

Bon Voyage

As we close *Strength in the Storm*, we hope the stories we've shared have touched your heart, inspired your spirit, and filled you with renewed strength. We believe the journeys and victories we've written about here will remind you the Lord is always by your side. Even if you currently find yourself in calm waters, life's challenges will inevitably come, just as rain clouds gather with consistency and certainty.

Even Jesus experienced storms. In one, He slept peacefully in a boat while the waves battered against it. When the disciples could no longer bear their fear, they woke Him in desperation, pleading for rescue. Jesus, always being calm and steady, rebuked the winds and the waves, commanding peace, and the sea obeyed. Just as He commanded the storm to cease for the disciples, He will do the same for you.

Know this: Jesus isn't pacing the halls of heaven, wondering if the storm will overtake you. He already knows when it will end. He sees you. He sees your struggles, your need, and even your desperation. He is at work, shielding you, guiding you, and holding you steady. He is your strength in the storm, and He will lead you to the still and restful waters.

Prayer:

O Lord, thank You for watching over this dear reader, for shielding her and keeping her safe in Your care. You are mightier than any storm she will face. Hold her close and grant her Your peace as she walks the path before her. We thank You for Your promise that no one and nothing can snatch her from Your hands. Keep her Yours, Lord. In Jesus' name, amen.